30 Day Setting up as a Virtua

First published 2012 by HLS

This edition published 2013 by HLS ı ....

www.trainingforvas.com

ISBN: 978-1477489833

Copyright © Helen Stothard

Introduction

Welcome to the 30 Day Setting up as a Virtual Assistant Challenge.

Taking the plunge from employment to being self employed can be scary; whether it's working out how to fund it, where to find the time, how to handle the objections and heckling from people around you, or wondering how you're going to sell yourself when you've never had to sell before.

I won't lie to you and tell you that it's going to be easy; in fact I can promise you now that if you do this properly you will work harder than you've ever worked before; but I can also promise you that this can be the best decision you will ever make.

Don't assume you have to go into this full tilt either; I started out on a part time basis and know many Virtual Assistants who start out on a 5 to 9 rota. Not everyone wants or needs to go full time, and the good news is that you don't have to if you don't want to.

This is your business (how good does that sound!) and you make the rules.

In 2010 I set up intelligentVA, an online resource for Virtual Assistants whether starting out or looking to improve on their already established business. This runs alongside my own successful Virtual Assistant business HLS Business Solutions which I founded in 2009.

This book will hopefully guide you through some of the key steps for starting up; after that it's down to you - the sky's the limit.

Good luck with your challenge!

Follow the challenge on Twitter with the hashtag **#30DayVA**

Helen

Praise for 30 Day Setting up as a Virtual Assistant Challenge

I am just in the process of starting up my own VA business, so decided to order the 30 Day Starting up as a Virtual Assistant Challenge. I could not put it down, so much useful information, written in plain English. It gives you all the info you need to be successful. It lays everything out step by step. I would have to say, after reading it through I am now even more existed about setting the business up than I was before I read it.

I WOULD RECOMMEND THIS BOOK !!!!!!!
Karen Daniels

I ordered this book as I have decided to become a virtual assistant utilising my skills and experience working in the events and business industry. I have experience of setting up a business, but I wanted a ticklist approach for keeping me on track for the virtual assistant element.

The book breaks down the process in manageable, achieveable tasks and it was a huge help in focusing my thoughts and research into positive actions for settting up my VA business.

I will continue to use the book as my bible for checking and rechecking I am on the right path!
Lucy Hooper

There are many books on the subject of becoming a Virtual Assistant, but this one breaks each area down into manageable 'bite-sized' chunks, and the fact that it sets a task each day really focuses the mind! It's easy to read and has loads of helpful tips and tricks. Would thoroughly recommend it.

Kerry Riley

This is another little gem Helen which I heartily recommend to anyone who may be setting up as a Virtual Assistant, or perhaps looking for ways to improve their existing business.

I found that the book provided me with a clear structure of set up tasks to complete, and it was great, not only because I didn't have to search all round the houses to find this detailed information and guidance elsewhere, but also to gain from your experience.

Being a bit of a techie tools girl, I also thoroughly enjoyed your A to Z of Small Business tools Helen!

Thanks again from a grateful virtual colleague.

Irene Brodie

There are many books out there written for those thinking of setting themselves up as a virtual assistant, but I would put this one at the top of my list in terms of relevance and hard facts. For less than £10 you are virtually (sorry about the pun) getting a course which will, if you follow it through, get you started in the business. Helen calls it a challenge, and a challenge it is. Don't expect a walk in the park. She makes you work, but encourages you every step of the way with a great sense of humour and an easy writing style.

Gennyds

I must say before I embarked on the process I was sort of lost in a cloud of where to start, but having read the 30 Day Setting up book I found this to be invaluable I wouldn't have had the courage to go forward without it. It's a must for all considering setting up as a VA!

Amanda

Praise for Helen Stothard's other books

The A to Z of Virtual Assistant Tools

"As a new VA just starting out (my website only launched in early Jan 2012!), The A to Z of Virtual Assistant Tools is a great book! It's opened my eyes to a great deal of tools and resources that I'd never heard of. I will be trying out a lot of them to see how they can assist me in my new VA business and hopefully this will prevent me needing to take time out to streamline my own tasks in the future!"

Tracey A Dixon, *Virtual Assistant, Amber Cat Admin*

"I have known Helen for quite some time and know that she is an extremely competent and useful colleague to know, especially when you need to find a resolution to help a client. This A to Z is an excellent guide not only as a reminder as to what is out there, but also if you need to check up on getting a job done effectively and efficiently. So whether you are new to business or have been around a while, then this a key tool to have on tap!"

Rachel Brett, Virtual Assistant, Arbor VS

"I purchased this book and didn't think that I would get much out of it being that I am based in NZ but I read and it is just brilliant! All the tips and tricks I have now integrated into my own business and would definitely recommend to any VA needing some guidance on the technology out there - then this book is a great tool for you!"

Carole Unkovich, Virtual Assistant

How to get started on Twitter and Generate Business

"I would highly recommend this book to anyone who uses or wants to use Twitter.

It is easy to read, explains things in simple terms and gives you instructions on how to get going so you are up and running in minutes.

Can be read in 30 minutes and you can apply what you read only seconds later"

Why should you become a Virtual Assistant?

Because you can!

As I've already said there is no better feeling than being your own boss. No more waiting for decisions to be signed off by head office, no more 'we've always done it this way' conversations when you suggest improvements, no more frustration and no more commute. You'll be amazed how quickly you adapt.

That aside here are some reasons why you should become a Virtual Assistant:

- Job Satisfaction – you're in control, all results are down to your own hard work

- Work/Life balance – work when you want. No juggling holidays with other employees, no more covering someone else's shift, no worrying about getting time off for doctor or dentist appointments; the flexibility to attend school sports day or just have a day off to have a coffee with a friend who's in the area

- Income – you control your income, no more working for someone else's benefit (you still have to pay the tax man of course) but now if you earn it then you keep it

- Variety – no two days are the same, and as you're the boss you get to pick and choose which projects you take on

- Clients – as with the projects you get to pick and choose which clients you want to work with, and working virtually doesn't mean you can't still build a fantastic relationship with them

- Respect – your self-respect will go through the roof, everything you achieve is down to you

Day 1 – What do I need to become a Virtual Assistant?

Probably not as much as you think. It's a common mistake to go out there and buy everything you see - remember, you're not stocking an office block anymore. You can buy equipment as and when you need it now, and you probably have the basics already.

- A good computer that isn't shared by anyone else – don't let other family members on it. You can't afford to risk the data being compromised or the machine damaged. It's up to you whether you go for laptop or desktop; we'll discuss where you'll work later on

- A printer – an all in one makes sense. If you can afford one go wireless; it's much easier and less clutter. But right now, we're just starting up so we can work with what we've got to avoid incurring any unnecessary costs.

- A 'phone – again we can work with what you have, later on we'll discuss the various options and their merits.

- Internet – a reliable internet connection (not dial up)

- A sense of humour – you're going to need it in the days ahead

- A dedicated work space – you need an area that is yours, with a door you can shut so you are not interrupted when you are working. If you have to start out in a corner of the dining room you can, but you won't be very productive

- A willingness to learn – don't think that now you're self-employed you stop learning. You're actually going to be in learning overdrive for the next few months, and you need to be prepared to continually embrace new ideas and new technologies

- A professional email address and domain name – we'll cover these later in the challenge as well

- Services - an idea of the services you are going to offer

- Support – you need support from the people around you

See, it's not as bad as you thought is it?

Challenge One

Today's challenge is to make a list of the skills that you have. I want you to put it into two columns.

What I can do
What I love to do

Just because you can do something doesn't mean you should, or have to. Remember, this is your business. You may find that the list of things you love offers enough scope on its own, but you may need to add in some of the tasks from the 'can do' list as well to make your Virtual Assistant business profitable.

I'm going to be cheeky today and get you to do another task as well; let's face it, as a Virtual Assistant you're going to be multi-tasking all the time anyway!

Your second part of the challenge is to write another list.

Reasons I will become a great Virtual Assistant
Reasons I shouldn't become a Virtual Assistant

We're setting out on a positive note hence the word WILL in the first list. You may find you have the same item in both columns, sometimes they can be both a positive and a negative.

I've said before, this is not going to be a walk in the park. I want you to start out on this challenge fully informed.

Day 2 – Virtual or On Site?

If you're reading day two then I hope the lists you did yesterday convinced you that you can do this and you're going ahead. That's great news.

Now we need to look at where you run your business from.

The word 'Virtual' implies that you will be working from your own premises. However, a lot of clients still like you to work from their office when you carry out work for them.

You need to decide now if this is something you're prepared to do. Let me remind you that this is your business and you get to make the rules. Just because you're setting up as a Virtual Assistant doesn't mean you have to be the same as everyone else.

I know some Virtual Assistants who always work from clients' premises, working somewhere different every day. I know others who only work from their own premises exclusively, be that home-based or a dedicated office. Then there are others who are between the two.

Does the list of services you are going to offer require you to be at a client's premises? Does the list mean that you can carry out all the tasks remotely?

Challenge Two

Today I want you to think about where you are going to work from. This is important. It also requires additional work from you depending on your answer.

Working from Home

You've decided to work from home, great. Now you need to find out if you can. If you're in rented accommodation check your tenancy agreement and find out if you are allowed to work from home. Most tenancy agreements forbid this. If yours does then contact your Landlord or Letting Agent and explain the type of work you will be doing and ask if it is possible. Just because it says no doesn't mean it means no.

If you own your home and it's mortgaged you'll need to ensure that the mortgage company doesn't have a problem.

You will also need to check with your Local Authority if you need planning permission. This depends on a number of factors but could include the number of visitors to the house, parking, deliveries and the inconvenience caused to your neighbours.

Either way you need to decide if you will allow business visitors to your home. From an insurance perspective it's better not to. We'll discuss insurance later on in another challenge.

- Do you have a dedicated space with a door you can shut?

- Do you have enough room for the equipment you will need?

- Do you have a reliable internet connection?

- Is there a hotel or similar close by to meet clients if needed?

- If you have children do you have appropriate child care available – you cannot provide a professional service if you have children running around in the background when you're answering calls for example, or you may have urgent deadlines that mean you can't make the school pick up. Consider these issues now and allow for them in your business plan to avoid unexpected problems later

- Would friends and family think they could just drop in for coffee anytime? You need to set out some ground rules now

Working from Clients

You need to set yourself some ground rules. Whilst you will negotiate each circumstance individually you need to have a basis to start from.

- How far are you prepared to travel? Work out time/distance rules.

- What hours are you going to be onsite?

- What equipment do you need on site and who will supply it?

- How are you going to get to the clients? Local transport or your own car? We'll cover the changes required to your car insurance in a later challenge. Do you have a backup plan if the car breaks down?

Working from a Dedicated Office

Today you're going to research local office providers.

- Are you looking for open plan or closed office?

- Do you want reception to answer your calls and handle your mail?

- Are you wanting to share an office with someone else?

- Can you have your own phone line and internet?

- Is there a possibility of gaining work from the other tenants?

- Is the space on offer available when you need it? Some offices have long waiting lists

- Is there access to a separate meeting room if required?

- Is the cost of the office within your budget? Explain you are just starting out and ask if they have any introductory offers?

- Arrange a visit to check out the space.

As you can see whichever option you decide on requires a fair amount of thought and planning in advance, but, again, it's your business and you can always change your mind later on.

Day 3 – Research

Today you're going to find out about other Virtual Assistants. Over the past few days we have decided what work we want to do and where we want to do it from. Now we are going to find out about our competitors and our target market.

The Virtual Assistant industry is growing worldwide, and thanks to cloud computing it is now within everyone's ability.

Challenge Three

Yes, you've guessed it, there's more than one part to today's challenge as well.

I want you to research other Virtual Assistants to start with. Bearing in mind that no two Virtual Assistants are alike I want you to find out who is offering a similar service to you. Don't just look at your local area, unless you have decided to only work from client premises, after all you're working virtually. I know Virtual Assistants, myself included, who have clients not only in different countries but also in different time zones.

You need to look at businesses offering the same set of services as you. Read their websites, see how much they charge, how they describe themselves, how they describe their services. We're going to be writing our own material later on in the challenge but feel free to make notes on anything you do or don't like, what works and doesn't work?

Now I want you to go back to the list of services you have decided on. Does a particular type of client stand out? Does your list of services look like it will appeal most to trainers, doctors, lawyers, accountants or builders, to name just a few? When you have identified at least two types of target client I want you to hit the internet and find them. What you're looking for today is an idea of where these clients 'hang out'. Do they have social media links on their websites? Do they use these social media sites? Is there one particular area that stands out? For example it may be that Lawyers tend to have LinkedIn in common whereas a builder may be more likely to use Facebook.

Again, if you're working from client premises then concentrate your research to your local area, otherwise look globally. Take your time with this challenge.

And there's more. I want you to take the research and see if you have a large enough potential client base when compared to the list of services you wrote out on day one.

Depending on the results you may find you need to expand your list of services, or you may decide you need to streamline them further.

Some people feel that clients prefer a Virtual Assistant who has a specialist niche as opposed to a generalist. A niche does make it easier to help you market yourself to your target market, but you may not know what your niche is just yet.

Day 4 – Name your business

Today we need to think about naming our business.

Stop... it's not that simple. There are several factors to take into account here.

- What niche are you looking to work in?

- Who are your main clients going to be?

- Does someone else already have the name?

- Does the name explain what you do?

- Can people spell your name?

- Will people understand your name if you tell them it over the phone?

- Will your name fit into a business card or letterhead or website banner?

- Could your name be confused with a different business or imply something other than that intended?

- Will your business name grow with the business?

Finding a name for my business was the hardest thing; I didn't want to sound like a one man back bedroom worker as I planned to expand the business one day. It also meant that I didn't want to use the words 'Virtual Assistant' as perhaps the business would diversify as it grew.

I drew up a shortlist of possible names and called on friends for their advice. I looked at words that would imply professionalism, and I considered where the business would show up in directories. I didn't want to be an A right at the front, I didn't want to be A1. I wanted something more.

I eventually settled on HLS Professional Services. A name that met the criteria I had set for myself. I promptly ordered business cards and domain names and found myself having to do it all again just weeks later.

I'd only asked a handful of people. I'd given them a shortlist to choose from without asking them what the name signified to them.

I then attended a Business Link training event, introduced myself and someone shouted from across the room that my business name made me sound like a hooker. The damage was done. Once that picture was in my head I couldn't get rid of it. The name had to go. Back to the drawing board and HLS Business Solutions was born.

Challenge Four

Today's challenge is to come up with a business name. I want you to spend time on this because some of the challenges we're about to come up with will need you to have decided your business name.

Go back to the lists you made yesterday, look at the type of services you think you will be offering and come up with a name that encompasses those services.

Your name shouldn't be:

- A misspelling of a common word – people just won't get it

- Complicated – it needs to be easy to remember

- Obscure – makes people think you do something other than what you're offering

- Common – try and be unique, you can always Google or check Companies House to see how many people are trading under that name already.

And yes, there's more! You didn't think it would be that simple did you? I want you to get feedback on your business name.

Satisfy yourself that your chosen name isn't on the list of things I've asked you to avoid and ask friends, family and more importantly business associates for their opinion.

Ask them what they think of when they hear that name, what they think the business does, how the name makes them feel. Note that I asked you to ask business associates as well. Don't base all your research on friends and family, especially if they're not self- employed.

You're looking for the AND now aren't you. The extra work I normally ask you to do, well I'll give you a reprieve today as I figure by the time you've completed the challenge I just set you it will be well past your bedtime anyway!

Day 5 – Find some support networks

No, you're not going to go rushing out today and buy everything with your business name on it. I want you to have a 'cooling off' period for a few days so you can play around with the name, see how it feels when you say it out loud, and give it chance to either grow on you or for it not to feel right.

Being a Virtual Assistant is great; there's a whole community out there ready to support you. That's right, I said support.

When I started out as a Virtual Assistant I was shocked by how helpful other Virtual Assistants were. I was confused. My experience was that small businesses didn't help each other, especially if they were in the same industry.

You know what? There's room for us all. The strength of the Virtual Assistant community is that they share, they collaborate and as a result it's an incredibly strong supportive community. You may be working in your office on your own but support is only a call or a keystroke away.

There are a lot of resources out there for new Virtual Assistants that can put you off. They'll want to charge you a fortune to become a member, or they'll want to exclude you if you haven't been in business for two years already. These are just a couple of examples I can think of that I came across.

Don't dish out the cash just yet. You may decide later that it's a worthwhile investment but right now look for the free resources available to you.

SVA - Society of Virtual Assistants

SVA has a special place in my heart as it's the first resource that I came across when setting up my Virtual Assistant business that, not only didn't ask me for money, but showed me that collaboration exists in the Virtual Assistant industry.

Their forum was a refreshing change; people were really sharing help and advice on what did and didn't work, and were happy to help another Virtual Assistant with product recommendations or just by sharing experience.

Caroline Wylie who heads up SVA is a smart cookie; she has built her own business and really has the respect of the VA industry. She's someone to look up to and admire. I purchased some of Caroline's time not long after my business went full time so she could talk me through her experience of working with associates and it was certainly money well spent.

SVA are also very active in promoting Global VA week in the UK, which normally takes place in May, organising and promoting events throughout the UK and online in a bid to promote the UK Virtual Assistant industry. It's thanks to them that intelligentVA now has regular coffee meetings as they asked people to host them locally around the UK and we enjoyed it so much we carried on meeting every month! http://www.societyofvirtualassistants.co.uk/

intelligentVA

http://www.trainingforvas.com is the home of the intelligentVA website. I couldn't write a book about becoming a Virtual Assistant without including this!

intelligentVA is an online resource for PAs and Virtual Assistants, whether they are just starting out or are wanting to take their business to the next level.

The site is crammed full of resources, training, tools and tips to help you move your business forward at a rapid pace.

The site's contributors are all experts in their relevant field, sharing their experience and knowledge. The blog is frequently updated with topics covering everything from starting out to marketing, sales and training opportunities.

IVAA - International Virtual Assistants Association

This is an international site that connects Virtual Assistants around the world. They hold online chats in different languages, organise virtual and physical events and have a newsletter ten times a year.

http://www.ivaa.org

Challenge Five

Today's challenge is to visit two of the sites mentioned above, and to go out and see which other support sites you can find. Spend some time in the forums and read through the blog posts. Most sites have interviews with Virtual Assistants so you can see what it's like for people like you who are setting up their own business.

Day 6 – Work out your rates

We've worked out what services we want to offer, we've researched our market and we've looked through the support sites. We should have the information we need now to start looking at our rates.

What we are NOT going to do is ask friends and family what we should charge. If they own their own business and want to use you they'll come up with a low rate and if they don't have their own business they'll base it on their own employed hourly rate.

As a Virtual Assistant you carry out the tasks yourself. This means that there are a finite number of hours you can work during the week. Don't think you can work a 40 hour week because it's not possible to do this and run your own business at the same time. I'm going to suggest that when you are looking at the hours you have available to work that you allow one day a week to carry out your own admin and marketing.

Establish the hours that you are able to work, excluding your admin time. You will need to take travelling time into account if you visit client premises. Now work out the amount you want to earn and divide that by the hours you have available. Great! Actually no, not so great. There's probably a load of things you haven't taken into account here.

- **National Insurance** – this works out roughly £12 month for your additional contributions

- **Self Assessment** – a very basic rule of thumb here is to put aside a third of what you owe to meet your tax bill

- **Insurance** – we'll cover this later but we're talking professional insurance, property insurance, vehicle insurance, income insurance and health insurance

- **Professional Memberships** – depending on the services you offer you may find you need to pay an annual fee, for example in order to offer bookkeeping I have to pay for my Money Laundering Regulations licence which is £110 year

- **Networking** – you may decide to join local networking groups or organisations like the Federation of Small Businesses

- **Utilities** – if you're working from home there'll be an increase in bills for heating, telephone, possibly internet and you will need to take these into account

- **Software Licences** – all the software you use must be correctly licensed. If you use cloud-based systems some of them will involve a monthly or annual cost

- **Office Equipment** – you'll need to buy stationery, replace computers as they wear out, buy a desk and chair etc

- **Travel** – do you have to travel to a clients' premises, a networking event or training or conferences, will you need hotel accommodation?

- **Childcare** – will you need to pay for child care?

This list isn't exhaustive. There are loads of things that you forget about when starting up a business, and whilst a lot of them are allowable business expenses, the business has to make a profit in order to pay you a wage.

Challenge Six

For today's challenge I want you to start thinking about your rates. We need to see if your business is viable before we start spending any money.

Take the research that you have done and taking into account the costs mentioned above I want you to start thinking rates.

In my opinion you cannot run a successful Virtual Assistant business if you charge less than £25 hour. There is also the question of perception. If you visit small business forums a common misconception about Virtual Assistants is that they are back bedroom hobbyists or cannot be trusted. If you're charging £10 hour or less not only are you unlikely to be able to run a professional or profitable business but what perception will clients have of you?

I assume if you're considering making the move to self-employment you have years of experience behind you. That experience is valuable. You're also going to learn some important new skills as you build your business. It gives you a whole new outlook on business, and you can share that experience with your clients.

Do not undervalue yourself. Charge an appropriate rate that will generate the income you wish to receive as well as paying the overheads and expenses incurred by your business.

Charge what you are worth. If you have a very specialist skill then charge the appropriate market rate for that skill.

Beware of barter arrangements. If a client offers you a service or product in exchange for your services look at it closely. Work it back to an hourly rate if you need to. I spoke to someone who had been offered a service worth £60 month. When we looked at the amount of work that was expected in return, it equated to less than £8 hour return. This was not a fair exchange. Whilst there were added benefits that you couldn't put a monetary value on, they weren't enough to make this a sound business decision.

Don't go in cheap. There's a temptation when starting out to offer low rates. If you must do this then ensure that there is a time limit on the offer, and make it clear that after this time your rates will revert to the standard rate. This avoids landing a client at the initial low rate that stays with you on that low rate for years.

Consider offering packages. Ideally you want your clients to buy a retainer. This is a set amount of work every month for a fixed fee. Generally if hours are unused during that month they are lost. However, the benefit to the client is that they are guaranteed your time during that period.

Another option to consider is pre-payment. This means that you have a more attractive rate for clients who purchase a set number of hours in advance.

Both prepayment and retainer are paid in advance of the work being carried out and therefore do not have the disadvantages of your invoice not being paid when the work has been completed.

Today I want you to come up with:

- Standard hourly rate for virtual work

- Increased hourly rate for onsite work – decide if you are charging travel time and mileage or if this will be covered in the increased rate

- At least two retainer packages

- At least two prepaid rates – for example block of 5 hours and block of 10 hours

- If your work is specialist then work out either a specialist hourly rate or project rate – if you are considering project rates double check your calculations to make sure this isn't working out below your standard hourly rate

Day 7 – Insurance

We've briefly mentioned Insurance over the past few days but this is what we are going to concentrate on today.

You still may not have made the decision about going ahead, but we need to know what the costs would be if you do.

There are different forms of insurance to consider:

Indemnity & Liability Insurance

This is essential and covers you against errors or omissions. You can get a quote online but remember, your business doesn't fit into a box unlike some others. I have found that it is best to pick up the phone and explain exactly the services you will be offering.

The agent can then prompt you for the information they need to create your quotation. This will depend on the services you offer. If you're offering bookkeeping this will be a different insurance requirement to that of transcription for example.

Car Insurance

You know when you insured your car for social, domestic and pleasure and going to one place of work? Well that isn't enough anymore. If you will be using your car for business then it needs to be covered under your car insurance. This applies even if you are working from home. If you are going to meet a client for coffee, attend a networking event or participate in training then you're using the car for business.

You'll probably find your existing insurer will cover this for a small additional premium.

Contents Insurance

Chances are that your laptop is already covered under your home contents insurance, but... you're using that laptop for business now and some insurers won't cover that. This might be the case with your car insurance as well. Talk to your insurer, remember at this point we haven't decided we're in business yet so we're just gathering quotes, and ask them what is and isn't covered and if any additional premiums would be required.

Income Insurance

From the Virtual Assistants I have spoken to this is the one that most of them miss. You're leaving the sick pay behind now; there are no in-service benefits now you're self-employed. What happens if you get ill? I'm not talking a common cold, I'm thinking any illness that will last six weeks or longer. If you're self-employed you won't be able to pay the bills or the mortgage.

Income insurance is an essential. Talk to a Financial Adviser; if you need an introduction I'll be happy to make one. It's the first thing I set up when I went full time self-employed and my Financial Adviser did the hard work in finding me an affordable policy with the right level of cover.

Health Insurance

If you're leaving a job that had private healthcare benefits you may want to get quotes for health insurance so that you are still covered.

Challenge Seven

Today's challenge, if you haven't guessed, is to gather the relevant quotes from the various insurers. Don't rely on internet quotes, pick up the phone to each of the insurers and get a detailed quote, and make sure you are aware of any limitations or special requirements.

- Indemnity and Liability Insurance

- Home Insurance

- Contents Insurance

- Car Insurance

- Income Insurance

- Health Insurance

Day 8 – Cash flow Projection

We've worked out our rates. We know how many hours' capacity we have each week and by now we should know our expected expenses.

We're going to write a cash flow projection to see what our business will look like over a period of months.

I did this for both a 5 to 9 business and a full time business in order to help me make the decision to go full time.

The beauty of a cash flow projection is that you can change one figure and the rest of the projection re-calculates automatically. This is an excellent tool for making sure your rate is correct. You can also use it to test what effect a special offer rate would have on your business.

Your projection works best as a horizontal spreadsheet. The specific items should be down the left-hand side and the months across the top.

The top of the cash flow is for your income. Break this down into clients, or tasks, so that the income is divided into categories. For example:

Balance b/f

Income

Client One

Client Two

Online Training

Commissions

Total Income

Now show your expenditure under the Income.

Expenditure

Insurances

Advertising

Telephone/Internet

Networking

Subscriptions

Travel

Salary

Tax & NI

Etc

Total Expenditure

Balance c/f

You'll note that I have shown Tax and National Insurance in this spreadsheet, you could include them in your salary. I like to show them separately as this way I can see if I have accrued enough in time to pay the half yearly bills.

At the far right of the spreadsheet you will have your totals. These carry over from the month before but this end column is the sum of the income/expenditure from all the months.

As you can see a balance carries forward to the following month. This could be a positive or negative figure. Because this figure carries forward, any amendments made to the content of the spreadsheet will affect the whole sheet.

Challenge Seven

Today I want you to write your cash flow projection in Excel. Drop me an email helen@hlsbs.co.uk if you'd like a copy of the template that I use.

- I want you to work out how much you will earn each month

- I want you to change your hourly rate or package rate and see how that affects the cash flow, is it better or worse

- Play around with the expenses and again see how this affects your cash flow

- Three months into your cash flow I want you to work out if you can buy a new laptop, is there enough profit in the business to do this? What happens if you wait until six months to buy it?

- Now you have played with the cash flow I want you to revisit your rates – are they going to work or do you need to make adjustments, particularly on your package/retainer rates?

Day 9 – Domain names and hosting

For some of you the words domain name and hosting may sound like a foreign language. Let me try and explain it in Helen speak.

The domain name is your identity on the internet; for now let's think of it as your car. It's unique to you and is what people type into their internet browser to visit your website.

Hosting is the space that your website occupies on the internet; this is your car parking space. You don't have to buy the domain and hosting from the same company.

You've had several days now to play around with your business name so today we're going to see if we can sort the domain name. It is very important that you don't look at this until you are ready to actually purchase, as sometimes your domain name searches are seen by people who buy domain names in bulk. If you don't buy it now they might, in the hope that they can sell it back to you at a later date for a premium rate.

You need to consider what you want your domain name to be, an exact replica of your business name, or something that links to your business name.

In the same way we had to think about the things that could go wrong with our business name we have to look at several factors when choosing a domain name.

- Avoid hyphens and underscores in your domain name if possible

- Keep it simple!

- Keep it short if possible – can you imagine typing in http://www.missmarplesinvestigativeagency.co.uk every time you want to visit the site? Is missmarples available? It still links to the business name without having all the extra. My website is http://www.hlsbs.com rather than the full hlsbusinesssolutions (it just looked like a recipe for disaster and mis-spelling with all those S in there)

- Do you want to have a .co.uk, a .com, a .info and the rest? If budget is really tight then buy the .co.uk which costs around £9.00 for two years, but, if you can, buy the .com at the same time so it's secured. A .com costs just over £11 per year. There are so many new domain name extensions available it can get confusing (the extension is the .co.uk or .com ending of a domain name) but bear in mind if someone doesn't know your domain name and is trying to work it out they may not consider trying some of the lesser known extensions (Check if your hosting company offers a free domain name if you purchase hosting from them, if I pay annually my host offers a free.com domain name).

- You don't have to do anything with it yet; buy it as soon as you know what you want and you can just leave it 'parked' until you are ready to use it

- Consider having a separate domain for your email and website. My website is .com and my email is .co.uk, this means that if one goes down for any technical reason the other should work

- If you can afford it you may wish to purchase an additional domain name that is more keyword related. For example, the website address of intelligentVA is http://www.trainingforvas.com which says what the site does. I also bought intelligentVA.com and .co.uk and these are 'pointed' to the website. This means that anyone using those domains goes to the correct website as I have redirected the traffic

There are a lot of companies out there who will sell you a domain and hosting. Don't rush in as you need to make sure of a couple of things first:

- Choose a company that will allow you to amend the DNS (domain name servers) as we will need to do this a little later on in our challenge to get our email to work

- Some companies offer a free domain name when you purchase hosting, this is great but do make sure that if you move hosting company the domain name belongs

to you and not them, as this could be an expensive
mistake

- Look for a hosting company that has one click
  installation for WordPress, we'll be setting up your
  website in it later in the challenge

- Ask for recommendations. Hosting especially can be a
  minefield. I use http://www.123reg.co.uk for my
  domains and https://www.evohosting.co.uk for my
  hosting. They offer a free .com or .co.uk domain name
  on certain packages and you can get a year's hosting
  for as little as £39.99 year, they also offer the one click
  WordPress installation

Challenge Nine

Today you are going to purchase your domain name. You don't have to purchase hosting yet but you will need it before the end of the challenge so do have a look at Evo Hosting. Ideally you can get a .com from Evo Hosting as your free domain name for your website and then buy a .co.uk version from 123Reg which we will use for your email account.

I'm not going to set you anything else today as I know how long it can take trying to find the domain name that you want! Just keep trying until you get the right one.

You may find that the name you want is available in .co.uk but not .com, this is okay, but... do check out who is using the .com; would you want people to land on that site in error when trying to find you? I'd much rather have a domain where I owned both the .co.uk and .com.

Day 10 – Setting up Google Apps

There is nothing worse than seeing someone in business using a Hotmail or Yahoo email address. Remember, earlier in the challenge we discussed perception? It's something I will keep talking about throughout the challenge. You are not setting up as a back bedroom worker, you are setting up as a proper business and need to be perceived that way.

I am also going to suggest that you really consider your existing email client if you're using something like Outlook. You're setting up as a Virtual Assistant. This means that provided you have an internet connection you can work from anywhere in the world! If you use Outlook then you lose that capability as you are stuck with the machine that it's installed on.

What happens if your computer dies? How quickly can you be back up and working again?

My suggestion, and of course it's up to you, would be to set up a Google Apps account from around £4 per month per user.

You may already have a Googlemail account but did you know you can get a Google Apps account? This allows you to have your emails linked to your domain name, share access to documents online, and even share calendars.

Gmail

I moved away from Outlook at the beginning of 2011 because I was tired of losing information when I changed pc and couldn't remember how to restore the backup file, or the pc crashed and refused to restore Outlook, but mainly because I wanted to access my email from wherever I was and for it to look the same and be the same. In other words if I hit delete on my phone I wanted it to delete on my laptop as well. I wanted one list of contacts, I wanted to be able to use my phone, netbook, tablet or laptop or even a friend's computer if I was away from the office. I'm not greedy, I just like to stay connected. Google allows me to do this. To start with I couldn't quite give up my Outlook folders so used the Outlook/Google sync tool that linked my email and calendar, but once I understood the 'labels' in Google there was no excuse not to make the move permanently.

My email now filters itself as it arrives, email relating to client A goes into a folder specifically for client A, newsletters go into a folder to be read later when I have time, certain senders go into an 'Urgent' folder, and there's even a filter for my daughter's school who now use email to communicate with me.

Calendar

Google calendar is an excellent tool if you wish to work virtually as you can allow access to other users, who can either view your calendar or view and edit. This means that as a Virtual Assistant you can book meetings on your client's behalf and they automatically appear in your client's calendar.

Another useful feature of Google Calendar is the reminder service. You can choose when you wish to have a reminder arrive and in what format. This means that you can not only book an appointment on behalf of your client but you can set a reminder to go to their mobile phone several hours before as well. Other options include pop up or email reminders.

Google Docs

If you have a document that both you and your client need to edit then Google Docs is an excellent idea, it allows for word and excel, albeit without a lot of the pretty formatting, and the best part of it is that you can both edit the document at the same time. It is kind of spooky the first few times that you do this but is so much better than trying to share a document via email, with different revisions. This way there is one document and all the changes are made on the one document.

Domain Name

Google Apps works on your domain name, the one we bought yesterday just for our email through 123Reg.co.uk.

As you go through the sign up process you will be able to create your personal email address that is linked to your domain name.

I have helen@hlsbs.co.uk, I also have accounts@hlsbs.co.uk for when clients send me receipts etc for bookkeeping. With Google Apps each user is payable, however, you can use alias email addresses at no extra cost. Both the helen@ and accounts@ email addresses come through to the same account. I can however add additional users for around £4 per month. This will be very useful later on in your business when you need to start working with Associates (an Associate is another Virtual Assistant who you subcontract work too when you have too much on, or if you don't have that particular skill).

Google Apps will guide you through the sign up process. You will need to log into your 123Reg control panel and make some changes but these are explained to you as part of the set up process.

Once your email has been set up you will be able to access your email via the internet, and download a shortcut to your desktop which will make Google work in just the same way your Outlook used to work.

When you decide on your email address don't go with the generic style such as info@ or help@, everyone does that. Use your name, it's more personal and more reflective of the type of service that you are offering your clients. In my opinion an info@ or sales@ email is the one that was given to the office junior as they hadn't yet earned an email address of their own.

We need to set up our email account today as we will need our email address quite often during the rest of the challenge.

Challenge Ten

Today's challenge therefore is to set up your Google Apps account.

http://www.google.com/apps/

Because you will need to carry out the amendments to your domain name this is the only challenge we have set for today. If you get stuck drop me a line helen@hlsbs.co.uk and I will see if I can offer any advice.

Day 11 – Get a VoIP 'Phone Number

I'm going to talk to you about perception again. Let's discuss your business 'phone number. If you see an advert with only a mobile 'phone number what does that mean to you? To me it means one man band who is never in the office. But wait, you say, you can use your home 'phone. True, but it's not a good idea. Do you fancy juggling calls with the rest of your household, the wrong person picking up the phone and answering 'Yeah' instead of your formal business greeting? Here's why I think you should get a VoIP phone number.

- Your phone number can be geographic so you can choose a number in your nearest large town – some people just outside of London like to be seen to have a London dialling code for example

- You could choose a non-geographic phone number such as 0845 but I don't recommend it. Many inclusive mobile phone and landline contracts do not include calling 08 numbers. This means that people would have to pay to call you instead of using their free minutes

- Your number is truly portable. I've seen businesses move from one side of town to the other and have to change their phone number because they couldn't transfer it. They were now on a different telephone exchange. This means that all the advertising they have done and issued is invalid. If they'd had a VoIP phone number it would have moved with them and they wouldn't have had to have everything reprinted

- If you want to you can divert the number to your mobile, no-one will be any the wiser. I did this whilst I was working 5 to 9. I answered my phone in my business name as the caller ID showed me it was an incoming business call

- You can easily divert your number to a call answering service, your home number or set it to go to answer phone (we'll discuss why you shouldn't let it go to answer phone later)

- You can set your working hours on your VoIP number

- You can have extensions on your VoIP number if you choose the right provider at the outset, you may need this later on in your business

- You can have inclusive call packages so that calls you make are at a fixed budget each month

- You won't be tying up your home landline

- You'll have separate billing to your home landline

- You can buy a dedicated handset and answer your calls on a proper phone (don't be tempted to use one of the free soft phone pieces of software and a headset, they are not reliable enough and we are trying to portray a professional image)

Again this is an area where you should ask for recommendations. I use two companies for VoIP. I started out with www.voiptalk.co.uk as they gave me a free geographic number when I took out a package which included calls. Latterly I have also used www.voipfone.co.uk. Voipfone has by far the more advanced service list including extensions, switchboards and even a 'call me back' button for your website (only use this when you have a proper VoIP handset and are there to answer the call).

When I started out I wasn't aware of Voipfone, and just needed to divert my line to my mobile or answer phone. When I was introduced to Voipfone they didn't have call packages although I now notice that they have started offering them.

Watch out for inclusive packages as you may find the cost of diverting to a mobile is not covered. I believe both sites allow you to pre-purchase credit which would cover this cost. Remember, most sites will allow you to upgrade your package, so you could always start off on a pay as you go basis and then upgrade once you know the scale of the service you require.

VoIP Handset

Most Virtual Assistants I know have purchased their handsets through Amazon. They're sensibly priced and have fairly quick delivery. They are dedicated VoIP handsets and come with their own router which plugs into the back of your existing router. Then like any other phone you can position them anywhere in the house subject to power socket availability.

One thing to think of here is whether you require one handset or more. I started off with a single handset but in hindsight would have been better off with a twin set. My office is two floors up and it would have been handy to have a handset in the main part of the house, although my handset is portable.

You don't have to buy a VoIP handset until you are ready. You can manage just by diverting your VoIP phone number to your mobile or landline.

As a rule of thumb you should be able to get a decent single handset for around £60.

Smartphone App

I am also able to make and answer my VoIP calls via my Smartphone thanks to a phone app. This means I don't have to invest in a standalone VoIP handset if I don't want to, and can answer my calls wherever I am. If you're an iPhone user then drop me a tweet or an email and I will let you know which app I am currently using for this. If you're an android user then search your app store for a Softphone application.

Challenge 11

Today I want you to research VoIP telephone number providers. Whilst some offer a free VoIP number there can be limitations such as:

- You can only have one number on the account – you may need to add additional phone numbers to your account as your business grows

- You are not able to transfer your number to another VoIP provider when you need to expand or change services or the cost is very high

- The cost of diverting calls is much higher than with other services

I want you to look at the two providers I have suggested and find another one of your own. I also want you to plan what you think you will need from your VoIP provider as your business grows.

You need to look at the cost of calls you will make, and find out how much it will cost you to divert your calls to your mobile or landline. Are these call charges included in any of the inclusive packages?

If you are in any doubt ring the sales team at the VoIP company and ask the questions.

This is an important stage in our business and we need to do the research and planning now to ensure that it doesn't become an obstacle to our business growth.

Day 12 – Create a basic WordPress welcome page

We have our business name, our domain name, our email address and now our phone number. Now we need a single page website. As your business grows you can add additional pages and information.

If you have purchased your hosting from the right company you will be able to install WordPress with a single click!

Don't install it into a sub directory if the option is offered. We want people to be able to find your website just by typing your domain name into their browser.

You need to log into your cPanel in your hosting account. You will have received an email from your hosting company containing a link to this.

You may find you have a pop up screen appear and offer you a video tutorial. Do use this if you're not familiar with cPanel.

Scroll down the menu until you get to the 'Software/Services' section.

In Evohosting there are two options to install WordPress, one called 'Installatron' and the other called 'Softaculous'. Either of these will be suitable.

If you have clicked on Installatron then scroll down to the content management section and select WordPress blog.

Click on install this application.

Your domain name will come up in the first box. Leave this alone.

The second box is called path. This is a folder that it is trying to create for you and we don't want. Whatever is in this box delete and leave it blank.

The install location should now show as:

http://www.yourdomainnamehere.com

Scroll down now to the Settings. Leave everything before this at default.

Change the admin user name and password to something you can remember and write this down now.

Make sure the email address for the administrator is your email.

You can leave the website title as 'My Blog' for now or you can put your business name in here.

Now click on install.

That's it, you've installed WordPress!

In order to access your website you need to enter your domain name followed by wp-admin in the address bar of your internet browser.

For example: http://www.mydomainnamehere.com/wp-admin

You will now see a log in screen asking for your user name and password, you wrote these down a moment ago. When you enter these you will be taken to your dashboard (it's like your control panel for your website).

The first thing we need to change is the theme. This is the appearance of the website. If you are a member of intelligentVA you will have been sent a free theme to use, otherwise you will need to search for a theme to install.

In the menu on the left you will see the word appearance, click on this then select theme.

Now select the tab at the top of the page that says install themes.

You can narrow your search down by colour, and a lot of other features or you can just click on newest or featured at the top of the page.

For now, we just need to find a theme that isn't the standard theme WordPress installs with. Installing a theme is not permanent. You can change it at a later date and not lose any of the content you have entered on your website. It's like changing your dress, it's still the same you underneath, it's just the outward appearance that has changed.

Find a theme that you like and click install.

Now click on activate.

Go back to the dashboard and go down to settings and select General.

In the site title box enter your business name.

You may not have a tagline yet, it's like a sub heading, you can leave this blank if you wish.

Make sure that the WordPress url and site url are the same as your domain name. Make sure that both begin http://www. and correct it if not.

Go to the dashboard and create a new page. Call this page blog. Publish this and go back to the dashboard.

Now go to settings and select reading. Next to front page displays select a static page.

Front page should be home and posts page should be blog.

Go back to the dashboard and select pages. Find the home page and edit it.

Replace the default welcome text with a brief introduction to you and your company.

Publish.

Challenge 12

Today you are going to follow the above steps and create a basic one page website for your business.

Now comes the interesting part. There are lots of free articles on the internet about using WordPress and I want you to find some and read through them. There are lots of tutorials.

I want you to learn how to add and edit pages and to read up on the difference between a blog post and a page.

Day 13 – Plan your website

A single page website is okay as a holding page but this is going to be our online brochure. For many people this is going to be the first time they come across us so it has to be right.

You need to think about the content and information you are going to share with your visitors.

As a rule of thumb you should display the following:

Home – this is the page they land on if they type your domain name

About – sell yourself to me, what experience do you have, what sort of person are you.

Services – what sort of service are you offering? Remember Virtual Assistants offer widely varying services; this is your opportunity to share your niche

Contact – how can they get in touch with you. This should include your name, a 'phone number, an email address and a physical address

Rates – some Virtual Assistants prefer not to display their rates, I prefer transparency. I also noticed that I got a lot fewer time wasting calls once I added this section to my website. The odds are that if someone has rung me they've already checked out my website and know what I am going to tell them. Rather than list an hourly rate I show a day rate.

Blog – this is something we will cover in more detail later but this is your way of sharing relevant news and information with your website visitors. It should be regularly updated

Testimonials – if you have any show them off! It's no good keeping them hidden away in a drawer or email folder

You've already researched other Virtual Assistant websites earlier in the challenge and made a note of what you did and didn't like. Can you incorporate any of the things you liked into your own site?

What we are not going to do is copy anyone else. Apart from being highly unethical we are unique, remember.

The other thing we are not going to do is bleat on about how we are cheaper than an office worker. Yes I know you don't get holiday pay or take up a desk or the rest of it but you're not an office worker so stop comparing yourself to one. You are a business owner offering a service to another business owner. If you're happy that you worked out your rates correctly in our earlier challenge then you won't have any need to justify them or compare them to anyone else.

What you are going to do is sell yourself. Yes, I know, it's hard work trying to big yourself up, and pretty uncomfortable too. Just start off small, remember, this is our website, we can edit and add to it as often as we like.

Challenge Thirteen

I want you to take a piece of paper and draw your website out today. Trust me, this is the easiest way to do it.

Start with your headings or page names and then write underneath what you want that page to do, what pages will link to it.

Once you are happy with the navigation of your site you can start to write the content.

Even if you only add one or two paragraphs to each page for now we need to get some content up on the site so that it doesn't look like you're a total newbie.

When you write your content do not say We, say I, unless of course you have a team of people working with you already.

Be honest about who you are, what you do and what you can offer a prospective client.

Add a call to action on each page – this is what you want the visitor to do when they have read the page, such as call me, email me or read more here.

By the end of the day you should have several pages on your website. This is now an ongoing challenge. Your website should be constantly updated and reviewed to ensure that it is always accurate and reflective of the services you offer.

Get someone you trust to give you feedback on the content and spelling. You don't want to lose customers because your shop window is faulty!

Whilst you are doing this initial stage of your website yourself, remember we are trying to set up here without breaking the bank? You can always talk to a professional designer at any point. You won't lose any of the content that you have already entered. You'll just get a shiny new showcase for your work instead.

Day 14 – Join Twitter

Don't panic! Keep calm and tweet on…

If you are serious about becoming a Virtual Assistant you need to be on Twitter. It took me a while to understand what it was, how to talk in 140 characters or less, and why I should be on it. If you're in doubt try reading my 'How to get started on Twitter and generate business' book.

Twitter is not about selling. It's about conversation. It's about learning. It's about sharing. The clients will happen if you follow a sensible process.

I cannot teach you Twitter in one day, it's not do-able, and, to be fair, like most things to do with my Virtual Assistant business, it's something I am still learning. I'm always looking for new ways to improve the systems and processes I use.

Be yourself on Twitter. People go on there for the people, not the business stuff. Talk about the things you enjoy, the TV you watch, the food you eat, even your children if you have them. Talk about your hobbies and interests. I have a lot of followers who love running, or just enjoy my tweeting about my own running; I have another set of followers who follow me because I have a good sense of humour; there's the local brigade who follow me because I live in York.

I have made some fantastic friends on Twitter and been fortunate to meet some of them for real. When you do make friends on Twitter and finally meet it's like you're meeting an old friend from school again, not like meeting someone for the first time.

It's surprising just how much of your personality can come across on Twitter, and when you are working virtually it's an excellent way of connecting with like-minded people.

As a general rule I would advise splitting your Twitter activity into three priorities.

- Spend the first third of your time tweeting about you as a person and have conversations

- Spend the second third of the time tweeting for other people, this means sharing with your followers information that other people have tweeted, be that tweets or blog posts, information about events, or even requests for help. If you see someone ask for help and you can, then do it. You may feel you need to keep all your trade secrets. That's not the case. Build a reputation for not only the knowledge that you have, but for your willingness to share that knowledge

- Lastly, and very lastly, talk about and promote your business. If people don't know what you do they cannot refer other people to you.

Challenge Fourteen

Today you are going to sign up for a Twitter account if you don't already have one.

- You can find me at:
  http://www.twitter.com/helenstothard (@helenstothard) and I want you to sign up with your name, not your business name

- Follow five new people today, this can include me but I want you to find four other people to follow. If you're stuck Twitter will suggest people for you to follow or you can see if you like any of the people we talk to

- Send a tweet using the hash tag **#30DayVA** so we can find you and say hello back

- Tweet that you are new to Twitter and you are looking forward to talking to people

- Send another tweet with a brief introduction about you

- I don't want you to protect your account – we want people to follow you and be able to talk to you and share your tweets

- I don't want you to set up an Auto DM, these are incredibly unpopular and lack originality

- I don't want you to sign up for any form of validation service, again these are very unpopular and only serve to prevent people following you

- I want you to research Twitter, there is a lot of information out there so just go and do a Google search.

- I want you to load a photo of YOU to your profile, and do it today, you don't want to be an anonymous egg

- I want you to write your kick-ass 160 letter bio. This is incredibly important and it's your image, bio and recent tweet history that a lot of potential followers will base their decision on

- I want you to include your shiny new website address in your profile

Day 15 – Write a blog post

Don't screech! It's not that bad – honest. I'm even going to tell you what to write about!

You need to decide a blog post length that is comfortable for you. For some people this is 300 words, 400 words or more. I'm a bit of a rambler so I tend to blog somewhere between 500 and 600 words; it's just what I find comes naturally.

A blog post can be an opinion, sharing knowledge, introducing people, writing a review; there's so much you can do

Challenge Fifteen

- Write a blog post about setting up your virtual assistant business

- In less than 600 words (your own words, don't make it sound formal if that's not you, write it the way you would say it as long as it contains correct spelling and grammar) share the good and the bad, what you have learned and what you want from your business

- Find a free photo from one of the photo websites such as http://dreamstime.com or http://www.photopin.com and make sure you show the relevant photo credit or

purchase an image from a site such as
http://www.fotolia.com

- Publish the blog post

- Tweet a link to your blog post and drop a link to
  helen@hlsbs.co.uk so I can leave a friendly comment
  on it for you

- Go back to the internet and research other people's
  blog posts. Again you're looking for things you like and
  don't like. Draw up a list of five things you found that
  you liked and five things that you didn't like. Next time
  you write a blog post use this list to improve your blog

- Write a blog plan – be honest with yourself, don't
  commit to blogging every week if you know you won't
  be able to do it but do have a regular schedule

- Write down five possible blog titles for future blogs –
  good ideas are
    o Five things I like about
    o My top ten tips for

Day 16 – Join LinkedIn

LinkedIn is a professional networking site. I suppose it's a bit like an online CV. As a Virtual Assistant it's somewhere you need to be seen.

You should have a professional photograph, a lot of people go for a head and shoulders shot and complete your profile information.

You shouldn't put 'owner' as your professional headline. This is a bit like your Twitter bio, it's 120 characters and your chance to sell what you can do.

Complete as much information as you can on your profile.

Challenge Sixteen

- Set up and complete your LinkedIn profile http://www.linkedin.com

- Make sure you include a link to your website and include your Twitter name

- Do not connect your LinkedIn account to Twitter. These are two different audiences and they don't want to see every tweet you make

- Look for people you already know on LinkedIn and send them a connection request; don't just send a generic request, personalise it: let them know you've just set up your account, you're setting up your own business and you'd like to be connected to them

- Think of people you already know who could write you a recommendation, I want you to send at least one request for a recommendation today, don't worry if they are not on LinkedIn as it will prompt them to join. LinkedIn recommendations carry more weight as they cannot be created or edited by you, only by the person making the recommendation

- Find one group that you want to join and introduce yourself. We have an intelligentVA LinkedIn group you are more than welcome to join
  http://www.linkedin.com/groups/intelligentVA-3906866

Day 17 – Set up a CRM system

You are going to need a CRM system to keep track of your contacts and manage your tasks.

You need to be able to record activity and ensure that a follow up is carried out. You may even wish to track pipeline activity.

Before you set up your CRM you need to plan it.

Here is a blog post I wrote last year to explain this in more detail.

Because I spend so much time working with CapsuleCRM I am often asked to help people set it up for the first time. There is a temptation to just jump in and import your contacts but my advice is hang fire and spend time planning your CRM system to ensure that you get the most out of it. The first thing you need to do before you enter any data into your shiny new CRM is to plan it out, use a mind map or piece of paper if you like.

By all means import that CSV file, but you may want to set it up first with the tags and custom fields that you will want to use going forward. If you haven't got a clue what I am talking about let me explain the difference between the two.

TAG

A tag is not individual to any person or organisation, it's simply a way of identifying them so that you can filter out the information at a later date using the list function. It's not unique. One record can have a multitude of tags. Examples of tags are:

Client
Supplier
Prospect
Name of your networking group
Name of event they attended

CUSTOM FIELD

A custom field is something that is unique to that record, be that a person or an organisation. A custom field is searchable in the search box as well. Again, you can use the custom field data to sort a list at a later date. A custom field can be text, a calendar date, a tick box, a selection from a drop down box but as it is something that can only be entered when you are editing the record it's best to use it for unique information such as:

Anniversary, Event or Start Date, Customer Number

Reason

So why are you getting a CRM system? Do you just want to use it as a souped-up address book or do you want to set it up so that it can work for your business going forward? What do you want to get out of it at a future date?

Users

Think about who will be using the system and remember that however well you design your CRM it is only as good as the weakest user of the system. If you make it too complicated people won't complete the fields and the data will be useless.

Reporting

What do you want your CRM to feed back to you? It can only give back what has been put in, and this is where getting the custom fields and tags correct is important. You will use both of these to generate lists at a later date so make sure before you set it up that your records are tagged before they are imported or you could find yourself spending an incredible amount of time correcting each record individually.

Importing

You can import your LinkedIn contacts, your Outlook contacts and pretty much any csv based list of contacts, but at the moment you cannot merge them at import. Put your lists together before you import and keep the record that has the most complete information. Edit the csv before the import stage so that it has as much data on it as possible. Create columns for the tags you wish to use in your csv. CapsuleCRM will create them for you if they don't already exist. You can create notes or background information in your csv file as well. When you import, CapsuleCRM allows you to map the fields to their system.

Useful Tips

- *Don't add Mr & Mrs, create a separate record for each individual*

- *Have separate columns for first and last name*

- *Put each line of the address in its own column, you should have at least line 1, line 2, city, county, postcode, country as columns*

- *Make sure you specify if the address is work or private*

- *Find out the LinkedIn profile address, Twitter ID, Facebook page address, Skype ID, Website address and Blog address as they are all available fields (Since this blog post was written Capsule now offers social media integration which searches your contacts and suggests the appropriate links)*

- *Background info is perfect for things that you need to stay visible on the screen of a contact record and not get lost in the note history; this could be information such as a customer's preferences, their wife's name, or even their customer number if you chose not to record this as a custom field*

Remember, you can always undo your last import so if you import the csv and realise you made an error delete the last import, correct it and start again.

If you use the integration available with MailChimp you can add subscribers or delete them from within CapsuleCRM (remember you must have permission from subscriber)

You can use the integrated contact form code from CapsuleCRM to have your website contacts sent direct to CapsuleCRM as well as your inbox.

Challenge Seventeen

Today I want you to sign up for a free trial of CapsuleCRM.

- Plan your CRM on paper

- Work out what tags and custom fields you wish to use

- Decide which contacts you want to import from your existing contacts

- Import the spreadsheet into your CRM

Day 18 – Write a Guest Blog Post

You've already written a blog post for your own site. Let's start to showcase your knowledge and experience on someone else's website. You get to include a small bio and your website link at the bottom of your guest post.

You should look for a website that caters for your target audience but isn't a direct competitor.

You can approach the website owner with a polite email requesting a guest slot, explain who you are, what you do and if possible include an example of the type of post you would like.

You could ask on Twitter if anyone is looking for guest bloggers on a particular subject.

You could email me as I have several sites that I post guest posts on.

Your guest post bio should be quite subtle, a short description of who you are, what you do and your website link. Don't go into a blatant sales pitch, this isn't your website.

Challenge Eighteen
- Contact two or three website owners that have suitable sites and request a guest blog position

- Tweet that you are looking for guest blogging opportunities on subject x

- Write your guest blog bio, keep it short and simple and no more than three sentences

- Prepare examples of posts that you have written to send to website owners

Day 19 – Set up your bank account

You can manage without a separate business bank account but you're just creating problems later on.

You need to keep a separate record of income and expenditure for your business. I have a business bank account, separate credit card for my business and a separate PayPal account. This makes it much easier to keep my accounts, rather than trying to filter out the personal transactions.

Your account doesn't have to be a business banking account if you don't want, but there's also no reason why it shouldn't be. Remember, we are setting up a professional business that we expect to grow.

If you're stuck for recommendations give me a call and I can introduce you to my bank contact, she's a lovely lady who has never let me down.

You should also start thinking about how you are going to keep your accounting records. A lot of people start off with a spreadsheet. I prefer to use a cloud based accounting system that allows me to create a pdf invoice and email it direct to the client; it also has a bank feed coming in direct from both my bank and PayPal, ensuring I don't miss transactions and making it easier to reconcile. It highlights when invoices are overdue and also integrates with my CRM system.

As with many aspects of your business; try and avoid a temporary solution. Go for a solution that will grow as your business grows; if you don't, you could find you outgrow your systems and processes and are too busy to research and implement new ones. If you start off with a system that will grow with you then this will not be an issue.

Challenge Nineteen

- Set up a separate bank account, preferably in your business name. Make sure you include your bank account sort code and account number on your invoices to make it easier for your clients to pay you

- Set up a separate PayPal account using your new email address and link it to your business bank account

- Consider having a separate credit card for business purchases

- Investigate various accounting systems and decide on the one you are going to use and set it up

Day 20 – Sign up with MailChimp

As well as having a website you are regularly updating with blog posts you will need a way of keeping clients aware of new services, important updates and other information that will be relevant to them.

Whilst this is classed as a Newsletter service it really is so much more. I have clients who have also used MailChimp to run email based training or managed events.

The A to Z of Virtual Assistant Tools that I have written originally started off as an email course with a different tool being emailed to the recipient each morning after they signed up to my newsletter. The idea was then developed further into a book which contained over 50 tools rather than the original 26. Whilst I wouldn't recommend an A to Z format (I struggled to find one example of some letters and had several for others) I do recommend using email courses to educate your list.

A list is a way of describing the people who have subscribed to receive your information. When I say subscribed I mean they have opted in. MailChimp has a very strong anti spam policy and as such you can't just send anything to anyone. You can only send mail to people who have asked to receive it. This is a common courtesy at the end of the day. None of us enjoy receiving unsolicited or spam email in our inbox, there's enough genuine stuff in there to concentrate on as it is, however, when you have the recipients consent and send quality information there isn't a problem.

You need to decide at the outset the following:

- How often you will send your newsletter, be consistent and regular

- What content you will include

- Only have one call to action in each newsletter in order to avoid losing the effect of your message – this is what you want your reader to do when they have finished reading your newsletter

- Do I need to have separate 'lists' for different areas of my business – you may have a list for telephone clients and one for social media clients rather than having a generic client list – it's better to send information that is specific to the recipient if possible, as they can choose to unsubscribe if your newsletter often doesn't contain information that is relevant to them

- The layout of your newsletter – whilst it's tempting to go for a multi column newsletter with lots of images are you sure you can generate that volume of content on a regular basis

- Whether you should have more than one template (design) for newsletters. For example I have a single column template with my logo for when I am sending out an announcement such as launching a new book. This only has one message in there so doesn't need to be a more complicated template

- What contact information you wish to include and whether to include a photo of yourself within the contact area

- What information will be static i.e. appear in the same place and say the same thing in every newsletter – this needs to be written into the original template to avoid having to re-create the content every time

- If you're referring to external content such as a blog post or website do you need to put the whole message in the newsletter or would it be better to have an excerpt and offer the reader the option to read more by clicking on a link

- What you are prepared to offer as an incentive for signing up to receive your newsletter – for example I have offered free eBooks, free training or a free email course and I have clients who offer a regular subscriber draw

- Whether you wish to include a competition in your newsletter – it's perhaps better to wait until you have a larger list before offering this as you may find with a small list you will generate very few responses

- Be prepared for people not even opening your newsletter when they receive it. MailChimp supply you with stats to show you who has opened your newsletter and if they have clicked on any links within the newsletter so you can see what works best for the next time. They also supply industry average stats so you can see how you compare to others within your industry

- Write a catchy headline – if you just see the word newsletter on the subject line in your inbox it doesn't really incentivise you to open it, however, if it's a news headline that catches the reader's attention then you have much more chance of your email being opened

- Who your target audience is. It's no good having a list of 1000 people if what you send out is only of interest to 10 of them. Like most things to do with your business it's quality not quantity that counts here

MailChimp could quite easily be a 30 Day Challenge all of its own (I may even get round to writing it one day) so today is just a brief introduction to the subject.

Challenge Twenty

Today I want you to sign up to MailChimp for yourself. Create an account. There are lots of free PDF guides on their website to show you how to do this and the following steps so I won't go into detail here.

Next I want you to give your list an interesting name as this will show up on the newsletter sign up form. Don't just call it newsletter. That said my newsletter sign up list is called intelligentVA or HLS Business Solutions.

I now want you to spend some time thinking about the following and writing down your answers:

- What style of newsletter do I want to send

- How many templates do I need

- What reward am I offering for signing up to my list

- Who I am writing for

- Read through at least two of the MailChimp guides as they cover everything from how to send your newsletter to the content you should include, one of them should include the how to section for setting up your sign up form

We'll cover creating your sign up form tomorrow and adding it to your website.

Day 21 – Create your MailChimp sign up form

Today we're going to create our sign up form. MailChimp allows you to create a really attractive template for your sign up form, very similar to the way you can personalise your newsletter template.

This is the first thing that prospective subscribers will see so make it an attractive proposition. If you have a logo then do incorporate it, but as we're starting out on a budget it's fine to just display your business name in a large colourful font so that it stands out.

Your logo or header should be at the top of the form. Underneath this please don't just write 'sign up to my newsletter'. Sell it to me, tell me, very simply and clearly, what's in it for me.

For example:

intelligentVA

intelligentVA
the resource for virtual assistants
who know knowledge is key

Check out our website for more useful information: intelligentVA the resource for virtual assistants who know knowledge is key

Sign up to our newsletter and get some free goodies from our training partner Sharp End Training including a LinkedIn Profile Builder, and webinar showing the '5 Classic mistakes VA's make', 'the biggest problems VA's face' and 'How to get prospects to call you'

The form shows the list name at the top, then my logo and underneath a link and description of my website. Below this is the 'bribe' advising what you get in return for signing up. You could also give more information on the sort of content that you will be sending out to enable people to make a more informed decision on signing up.

For example:

Our newsletter contains tips and articles that help you grow your Virtual Assistant business. Our contributors are all experts within their field and share with you their best practice ideas.

When you design your sign up form keep it as simple as possible for the subscriber. Do you really need to know everything about them or will a name and email address suffice.

My newsletter sign up form can be found here: http://eepurl.com/dP692

When you create your sign up form you have the option to share it, using the link above, or to embed it into your website. You need to know that if you embed it in your webpage you lose all of the design you have just carefully created as it assumes the design is already there within your website theme.

The simplest way to share your sign up form is using the short website link that MailChimp provide. If possible include this in a widget on your website so that it appears on every page, or at have a static page in your menu so that wherever the visitor is on your site they can see an option to subscribe.

Whichever option you choose to display make sure you include your 'bribe' so that subscribers know, before they click the link or choose to subscribe what's in it for them.

Challenge Twenty One

Today you need to set up your sign up form. You go to the list you created in MailChimp yesterday and select forms. Edit the sign up form and decide how you wish to integrate it into your website.

If you don't know how to do this you can always drop me an email, or better still, you can do the research on the internet to find out how to do it. Use the guides in MailChimp.

Day 22 – Let people know what you are doing

If you're this far into the challenge it's a fair bet that you are going ahead with your Virtual Assistant business and you are going to need to find some clients soon.

People will not just appear as if by magic. Finding clients is one of the hardest, and from talking to a large number of Virtual Assistants, the scariest part of your business.

You need to let people know that you are available, you also need to let them know what services you will be offering. It's not enough to say I am a Virtual Assistant as many people have never heard of one, and those who have will know that it covers a multitude of services. In all reality I don't think any of the Virtual Assistants I know offer exactly the same service as a competitor. There may be many areas of similarity, but there are also many areas where they differ.

Go back to the list of services you created back at the beginning of the challenge. Have a quick review of it, after all you've had a few weeks to consider it some more, and then let people know you're here and you're available.

What you mustn't do is go out there and sell, sell, sell.

I know you think those last two sentences contradict each other, trust me though that there is a way to do this.

The people you are going to be talking to are not your prospective clients, although you may find they require your services. They are people you are going to have a quick chat to and ask for their advice.

One of the things you will quickly learn as you set up your business is that no one likes being sold to. Come to think of it not many people actually enjoy selling.

I want you to think about how you would react if you walked into a room and people started throwing their business cards at you before they said hello, or how you'd feel if you were meeting an old friend for coffee knowing they were going to try and sell you something. You wouldn't like it.

What you need to do is let everyone, and I mean everyone, know about your new business, at the same time reassuring them that you're not looking to them to buy your services.

"Hi Jim, I was wondering if you could spare me some time this week for a coffee? I'm setting up a new business and I would really value your advice and input. I need to let people know that I am available and what I do and would appreciate you helping me write my introduction."

You've now flattered Jim by asking for his advice and you've reassured him that it's just advice you're looking for.

Once you have your meeting with Jim you can let him know what you can do and the sort of people you would like to work with.

It could be that Jim actually requires your services, if so that's great, but more likely Jim may know someone who could use you and be willing to offer an introduction.

However, if you don't talk to Jim and let him know what you are doing, that contact he knows will never find out about you.

Now doesn't that sound a lot easier than selling? You're just having a chat with an old friend or work colleague over a coffee.

Challenge Twenty Three

I want you to select at least ten contacts to have this conversation with. I also want you to not assume in advance who will be a useful contact. You don't know who they know and should never make assumptions in your business anyway.

Now you have selected ten people I want you to call at least two of them today. That's right, no time to procrastinate or come up with excuses. Call at least two today.

This is really an ongoing challenge as you need to ensure that your network of contacts is aware of what you are doing and what you are capable of. A lot of my wider circle of contacts know that I am a Virtual Assistant, but it's only when I sit down and chat with them that they understand what that actually means and what I can do.

Now have a look at the people you connected with on LinkedIn earlier in the challenge. Is it worth having a call with them as well? They will see from your profile that you are a Virtual Assistant but may need you to explain to them what that means.

Oh, and so today isn't too easy for you I want you to nip on over to FreeIndex and sign up for your free account and list your business so people out there on the internet know that you are available for business as well.

http://www.freeindex.co.uk

Day 23 – Create a Facebook business page

Love it or hate it Facebook is here to stay and you need to have a business presence on there. I don't mean share your personal Facebook page with people; that should be kept separate for family and friends. You need to have a business profile.

You can visit an existing page on Facebook and use the create page link from there; or you can create a page from the Facebook log in screen. At the time of writing this can be found under the sign up box, although it does sometimes move.

When you go to sign up for a page you are presented with several different page types. It is important to get this right now, as there is no opportunity to change it later.

- Local business or place

- Company, organisation or institution

- Brand or product

- Artist, band or public figure

- Entertainment

- Cause or community

If you select the local business or place then you will appear on a map and be able to set your opening hours.

Select Local business or place and then choose Business Services from the drop down menu.

Enter your business name, followed by your business address information.

Make sure that you choose a suitable image for your business page, ideally a professional photo of you or your business logo and fill in the information page.

You may wish to feed your blog from your website into Facebook, this is a great way of populating your Facebook page with regular information. 'RSS Graffiti' is a useful Facebook application that will do the hard work for you.

It is possible to connect your Facebook page with your Twitter account but I wouldn't recommend it. The two systems have different audiences and what is suitable for one is not necessarily suitable for the other; nor will an out of context tweet make much sense to a Facebook reader.

What you can do however, is to give your Facebook business page a unique URL. This is a website address that is unique to your business page, and one that you can link to from your WordPress website, in your email signature and also on your business card. You can do this by visiting:

http://www.facebook.com/username

But stop! Before you do this – think very carefully about it. Once you have set your unique user name it cannot be changed. Make sure that this is the right name. Remember, earlier in the challenge, we discussed how you may need to re-think your business name? You don't have to decide on your unique Facebook url just yet. It may be worth waiting a couple of weeks to make sure you are totally happy with the name before you commit to it. Apply the same logic to the unique url as you did to choosing your domain name. Is it easy to type, can people find it easily etc.

A Facebook business page is not used in the same way as your personal page, and you certainly should avoid any content that could be construed as un-professional. However, you can post content that you have found useful on other websites.

For example, when I am reading the news each day, I often post a relevant article onto my Facebook business page, if I feel that it would be of interest to my Facebook followers.

As with Twitter, Facebook is not a numbers game. Whilst it is flattering to have a huge number of followers, it is better to have followers who contribute to your page, rather than just numbers.

Challenge Twenty Three

Today I want you to create a Facebook business page for your Virtual Assistant business.

I want you to connect your existing Wordpress blog to your Facebook business page using the 'RSS Graffiti' app which you can search for on Facebook. This should pull over your existing blog posts.

I want you to invite the friends that you think would be genuinely interested in your page.

Add a social media widget to your WordPress website and include a link to your Facebook business page.

Send a tweet with a link to your new Facebook business page inviting your Twitter followers to 'like' your Facebook page.

Lastly, I want you to find a relevant article or news piece that you think would be of interest to your potential clients and post this on your Facebook page.

Day 24 – Write your 60 Second Pitch

Whether you decide to attend physical networking events, or just stay online, your 60 second pitch is something you need to think about. Also described as an 'elevator pitch' this is how you sell the benefits of what you do to a stranger. You may argue that you don't plan on attending networking events, however, you should remember that you need to be able to explain what you do, at short notice, anywhere, anytime.

Whilst your pitch is effectively you 'selling' your business, ideally, we don't want you to talk about you. Sounds confusing doesn't it.

In just a few sentences you need to show how what you do benefits your clients.

So instead of saying 'I am a Virtual Assistant' think of other ways you can phrase this; ways that would actually make the person you are talking to think that you could help them as well. Make it sound interesting, and make it clear what the benefit is to your client.

For example, a web designer I know uses the following phrase:

'We help our clients build and maintain an attractive, effective online presence'

That sounds much better than 'I am a web designer' doesn't it! He is selling the fact that he cares about his clients' getting results from the site that he builds.

Take a look at the list of the services that you offer. Whilst some of them may seem run of the mill to you, remember that they may carry a great deal of weight with your clients.

As you are starting out you may not be able to give a 'case study' example. This is a specific example of how you have helped a client overcome a particular problem, and what that meant to your client.

'**I work with my client's to explore the different ways Social Media activity can benefit their business'** is one example that I could offer. If I need to go into more detail I could explain that client's rarely grasp the full functionality of a product like MailChimp, an online newsletter system; and that by working with them, we can create 'products' that they can market. We can then build on these products to establish the clients' knowledge and experience within a field as a pre-cursor to them then publishing their own book.

It is obviously better to have several different pitches prepared. Ideally let the other person introduce themselves first. This way you can come back with the introduction that will mean most to them. What I mean by this is that you wouldn't introduce yourself to an Accountant perhaps, in the same way that you would introduce yourself to a coach or trainer. The phrasing you use will be slightly different.

You need to practice your pitch until you are comfortable with it; it needs to sound natural when you say it. Don't be afraid to tell people that you are new; but do share with them the breadth of experience that you have. It's okay to have only just set up your business.

You need to try and answer the following questions in your pitch:

What you do? – we provide
Who you do it for? – for coaches and trainers
What's in it for them? – so that they can
Why you are different? – as opposed to
What your company is? - my company is an insurance against

The reason they call them a 60 second pitch is so that you keep it short and sweet. Focus it on what you can offer a client and don't go on and on.

Challenge Twenty Four

Today I want you to write three different 60 second pitches describing your business. In each one showcase a different product or service that you offer and explain how that is beneficial to your client.

Then fire them over to me helen@hlsbs.co.uk as I would love to read through them.

Day 25 – Go Networking!

Yes – you read that right! Now I appreciate that some of you may live in remote locations and struggle to attend a physical networking event. That doesn't mean that you can't network.

There are different ways of networking online. It could be having a Twitter conversation, becoming a member of a Facebook or LinkedIn group or joining an online forum.

Whichever form of networking you decide to take part in, the most important thing to remember is that you are not selling! Networking is about building relationships in the first instance.

Introduce yourself by all means. Show interest in the people you are networking with. Find out who they are and what they do.

I have attended networking events where people have come in, interrupted the conversation I was in the middle of, and thrust brochures at us along with business cards. This is not networking. It's blatant and it's rude.

I personally choose not to 'sell' when I introduce myself. Some of the meetings I attend allow you to take it in turns to introduce yourself to the rest of the attendees. I never say I am there to gain new clients; I am there to increase my network of contacts and hopefully to find new suppliers. This approach means there is always someone who wants to speak to me. What it also means is that I have found several new suppliers who are of benefit to my clients. A side effect of these networking events is that someone there, or someone they know, may require my services. Because I have not gone into 'hard sell' mode I have more chance of being remembered for the right reasons.

Whether you are networking online or offline share your experience and knowledge. This is especially important in an online scenario. If you know the answer to a question then share that answer. If you believe a particular product or system will be relevant share that knowledge.

Day 26 - Install GetClicky on your Website

Over the past few challenges we have created your website, created blog posts and content, but we have no way at the moment of measuring the effectiveness of this.

There is a fantastic free tool that will help us do this on a 'live' basis.

You need to sign up for your free account first:

http://www.getclicky.com/

Monitoring the traffic to your website is known as Analytics. You may be wondering why this is important. You need to know what your visitors are looking for when they visit your website. You need to know what search phrases they are using, and then look at whether you are satisfying the search with the relevant information.

You need to know where your visitors are coming from, are they typing the address directly into the browser, or are they coming from a different website by clicking a link.

Once you know the answers to these types of questions it will help you with your marketing. You will know what content attracts the most visitors, as well as which content attracts quality visitors.

So what's the difference between a visitor and a quality visitor? Well it sounds good if you get 1000 hits a day on your website doesn't it. But what if, out of that 1000, only 5 people venture beyond the page they land on? You may have 1000 visitors but in actuality only 5 of them would be quality. What you need to try and do is write and publish content that attracts visitors to your site, and then they stay, and look at other areas of the site as well.

One statistic that helps you know whether they are finding relevant content is the bounce rate. This is the percentage of visitors who click off your website as soon as they land because the content was not what they were looking for. An example of this is someone arriving on your website because they searched for central heating. They have been sent to your website because the content uses the phrase central heating. However, you are not the central heating expert that they were looking for, you were just writing about a client who specialises in central heating. You're not what they are looking for so they leave. This is a bounce.

Now of course, there is a whole science behind website traffic, search engine optimisation (SEO) - this means that your website attracts more search engine traffic, and the like. We can't possibly cover that in our 30 day challenge. What we can do is introduce you to the GetClicky tool that will help you work out what is working and what isn't working in terms of your website traffic.

The next part of the set up process is to go add the WordPress plug in to your website. Of course, it's not as easy as typing in GetClicky to find it. It's called 'Clicky for WordPress' and is written by Joost de Valk.

Once you have added the WordPress plug in you are up and running.

You can now tweet a link to your website, log into the GetClicky website and you should be able to see people landing on your site. The stats in the top right of the page show you how many people are online right now, how many visitors have been on your site today, and how many actions those people have taken. (There is an app you can pay for so you can monitor this via your iPhone if you wish).

For example, one person online means one person is actually viewing your website right now. 10 Visitors means that over the course of the day 10 people have visited your site. 16 Actions means that they have clicked 16 times. This could mean that one person clicked 7 times and the other 9 only clicked once. If you want to know more information about what each visitor did you can drill down in to the various reports.

Challenge Twenty Six

I want you to open an account with GetClicky and install the WordPress plug in.

I now want you to post a link to your website either via Twitter or Facebook. Now go to the GetClicky website and watch the traffic arrive.

I now want you to really find your way around GetClicky, check the various reports and drill down.

As this will take quite a while for you to play with I'm going to make that your only challenge today - how kind am I!

Day 27 – Write Another Blog Post

Today I want you to write a new blog post. It's nearly two weeks since you last wrote one probably, and ideally, I'd like you to publish on a weekly or twice weekly timetable so you are constantly supplying your audience with fresh content.

You need to show your audience that you know your topic and share your experience.

This could be by sharing a 'how to' tip, writing a case study showing how you solved a particular problem (people like these if they can relate to them and identify with the problem).

Go back to day fifteen and look at what we talked about in terms of potential titles and content.

Make sure that you have a clear call to action in your blog post. What do you want your reader to do when they have finished reading your blog post?

Challenge Twenty Seven

As I have already mentioned, today you are going to write a new blog post and publish it.

I want you to tweet your blog post link, mention it on Google+, share it on Facebook and mention it on LinkedIn.

Now I want you to look at your website statistics that we set up yesterday on GetClicky. I want you to investigate at various times during the day and answer the following questions:

1. Which link generated the most traffic to the website?
2. Which link generated the most quality traffic to the site and why?
3. Which link generated the most actions on the site?

I want you to think about these answers and see if you can use the information you have gathered from them when writing new content for your site.

Is one link generating better traffic than the others? Why not try changing the information you send out in the link today and see if that makes a difference to the traffic and activity.

This challenge is not one that is over and done with in one day. This is something I want you to check at least on a weekly basis. It's not just checking it either, you need to react to the information you are obtaining from the traffic results.

Day 28 – Write your Marketing Plan

I know you are only just setting up but you do need a marketing plan. Even more importantly, you need to stick to your marketing plan.

Now don't panic and think I am suggesting you embark on expensive ad campaigns. I would hope by now you realise that I only suggest spending money when you can afford it and when it is justified.

Marketing is not just about advertising. Marketing is everything that you do to make people aware of your business. We've covered various aspects of it over the various challenges including Facebook, LinkedIn, Twitter, Networking and Newsletters.

Marketing is you telling people what you do and what you can offer.

If you have a budget that you can spend on marketing you need to make sure that it is written into your cash flow projection. I know a lot of companies who never allow for marketing when they write their budgets and react to situations depending on the cash flow at the time.

Look at the various events that take place in your area. Are there conferences you need to attend? Trade shows you could attend as an exhibitor? Networking events you can participate in? Write all of these into your marketing plan.

Next look at the costs that are involved with each event and ensure that they are in the relevant month on your cash flow projection and that, most importantly, you can afford to participate.

Now look at when you should start promoting your attendance or participation in these events. What do you need to take with you? Business cards, promotional materials etc. You need to ensure that you order these in sufficient time and at a time when you can afford to purchase them.

Now plan your blog posts, tweets, and Facebook mentions for before and after these events. Do you need to send out a press release before or after the event? Ensure that all these dates are included in your calendar.

Look at the blog topics you wish to cover over the coming year and add these into your marketing plan, along with the frequency that you will blog at.

Decide on the frequency of your newsletters and have a rough idea what theme/topic you will have for each one.

Look at the list of events/activity you have already considered and see where you can incorporate these into your blog posts and newsletter activity to complement your marketing message.

You may wish to use video marketing to advertise your business. Again, include this in your marketing plan.

Look at your social media activity and plan this into your marketing plan. Whilst you may be using free resources and social media sites you really need to consider the time you will need to make available to utilise them properly. After all, while you are marketing your business you are not earning money, so even a free resource or activity is still a cost when you take into account your non fee earning time.

Challenge Twenty Eight

This challenge will take several days to do, and should be regularly reviewed in order for it to be of benefit.

I want you to write your marketing plan, and to review it on a monthly basis. Don't be afraid to adjust your plan as you go along, you will learn what works for you and what doesn't.

Day 29 – Review your Website

Your website is one of the most important advertisements for your business. You need to review this on a regular basis. The longer you are in business the more you will find that you adapt. For example, I no longer carry out the same tasks I did when I started my business. The work has changed to reflect the new skills I have learned; it's therefore important that my website reflects these changes and I am not advertising services I no longer wish to provide. It will also do me no good if the new skills I have learned are not mentioned on my website.

Read back through the content you have written for your website.   After the last few challenges you may find you wish to revise the content slightly.

Ask other people to review your website for you. Can they find what they would expect to find on this type of website? Can they spot spelling mistakes or grammatical errors you may have overlooked?

Quite often when you come back to a piece of writing several days later, with fresh eyes, you realise you need to change something, or it doesn't quite say what you wanted it to.

Again, over the past few challenges you will have become more familiar with WordPress and installing plug ins. You may now wish to add some content to the side bars on your website, perhaps a poll or survey question, or links to your social media accounts.

Challenge Twenty Nine

Now here is a surprise - I want you to review your website! That's it for today, I think I've pushed you hard enough over the last twenty eight days, and besides, today is the day I want you to really think about what you are going to do. Look back over the last twenty eight days carefully because tomorrow you will make your final decision about this business, and if you decide to go ahead we're going to be talking to the HMRC and setting you up as a legal business.

Day 30 – Register with HMRC!

Hurray, you've made it to day 30! Well done.

Hopefully over the last 29 days I've set you enough challenges to have helped you make the decision about whether you are going to go for this or not.

Now regardless of whether you are going to do this full time or part time you need to register with HMRC as self employed.

http://www.hmrc.gov.uk/selfemployed/register-selfemp.htm

You need to register with HMRC sooner rather than later. Their website will guide you through the implications of registering with them and includes the online forms that you need to complete.

Once you become self employed, even if you are employed full time elsewhere, you will need to complete a self assessment tax return.

If you don't register with HMRC you may have to pay a penalty.

As well as registering as self employed you will also need to arrange to pay Class 2 National Insurance contributions. You may find that you will not earn enough from self employment to pay these additional contributions. If this is the case you will need to apply for an exemption certificate. If you do qualify for these additional contributions you can arrange to pay them monthly by direct debit, however, remember, these are not a business expense and cannot be claimed as such.

If you have any questions about self employment then do talk it through with HMRC. They have been extremely helpful to me.

You may be trying to decide whether you should be a self employed sole trader, or whether you should set up as a Limited Company, in which case you would be a Director of the company and be paid a salary. This would mean you also need to register with HMRC as an employer and pay PAYE.

I can't make that decision for you. Talk it through with an Accountant. You will also need to discuss with them whether you wish to become VAT registered.

The Accountant that I spoke to advised me to become Limited only if my turnover exceeded a certain amount, or if I chose to become VAT registered.

I did buy my limited company name in order to protect it for a later date. This means that I had to pay a small set up fee followed by an annual return fee to Companies House to declare the company as a dormant company. What I didn't do was pay someone else several hundred pounds to set that up for me. Again, talk to your Accountant about this.

Challenge Thirty

Congratulations, once you've registered with HMRC you are on the route to self employment in your own Virtual Assistant business.

The second task is to arrange to pay your Class 2 National Insurance contributions or apply for your exemption certificate.

And the last, but easiest of all tasks, is to finally sit back, kick off your shoes and celebrate with a drink! You're now a Virtual Assistant and I wish you every success with your new business!

Appendix

Cash Flow Projection

For a copy of the Cash Flow projection spreadsheet we mentioned in the challenge please email helen@hlsbs.co.uk

Blog Posts

The following articles were all written by me and have been published on the intelligentVA website over the last two years.

Who's Watching Your Back?

Being a VA is a great feeling. You are your own boss, an entrepreneur and responsible for your own success. However, it can also be a lonely feeling sometimes. But it doesn't need to be. By aligning yourself with other like minded individuals you strengthen your offering in more ways than one.

Being a member of the VA Support Group (VASG) is free. But it is worth its weight in gold. The group has around 80 members now from all backgrounds and skill sets. Whenever you are searching for the answer to something that is perplexing you then odds are someone in the group knows the answer.

The group acts as a virtual water cooler, you can pop in and out just for the company if you like, you can rant, celebrate, commiserate or advise. One of its best features is the speed of the response, as it is Skype based the reply is often instantaneous. It's kind of like turning round in a traditional office and asking if anyone can remember how you ...

Now whilst it is great being your own boss and being a sole trader that does put you in a bit of an awkward position.

What if you get ill? What if you have more work than you can handle? What if you have a family emergency? What if you want to go on holiday?

If you plan properly then none of these should be an issue. Quite often there is someone there who can help to take the strain, and can ease the workload over these trying times. After all if you are self employed and not working then you simply don't get paid.

One answer to this predicament is to talk to us at HLS Business Solutions. The core members of my team are VASG members, we all have the same ethos and mind set and work really well together as a team. They have been invaluable to me over past weeks when I suffered a devastating and sudden bereavement just before a family holiday. This meant I wasn't around for most of a three week period. Thanks to my team my Clients were properly catered for, my calls were answered and they never got in touch with me once on my holiday!

You don't have to be a VA to need this sort of resource or back up however, it applies to any sole trader.

Take a look at your back up plans. If you are suddenly unable to work who will look after your Clients? Start planning now while you are fit and well, look at working with a colleague to offer mutual cover, or talk to us about how we can help cover your holiday or emergency requirements. Look at your competitors who have similar skills so that you can cover for each other - adding to the collaboration not competition ethos. Rather than competing against each other both businesses become stronger for the collaboration. The trust that is built up is invaluable.

It's not just work load you need to consider, how many of you have made financial provision? One of the first things I did when I went self employed was to take out income protection, I didn't know what was around the corner, none of us do, but should ill health get in the way at least I know I can still pay my mortgage and keep the roof over my head. (If this is something you need to investigate drop me an email and I can put you in touch with an excellent Independent Financial Adviser who sorted my cover out).

So stop thinking sole trader and start investigating how you can take your business to the next level by working smarter not harder with other VAs.

From 5 to 9 to 9 to 5 and then some!

Blog post written in September, 2010.

Not many people know that just 18 months ago I was working for someone else. They think my business is older than it is, and I will take that as a compliment. 18 months ago I was working full time and received the unwelcome news that I either cut my working hours or face redundancy. Bit of a Hobson's Choice that one! I was being asked to work a four day week and had a mortgage and bills that required a five day income.

Who would employ me just one day a week? The recession had already kicked in, everyone was in the same boat, and many had already been made redundant. The employment agencies couldn't help me. Trying to find employment one day a week just wasn't something they could accommodate, they could handle temping, they could handle full time placements, but one day a week was out of their comfort zone. This was something I would have to resolve on my own.

I had a vague idea that people could work from home for others, I didn't know what it was called though, and I didn't really know what it could cover. So off to Google I went. I also chatted with friends and family and asked their advice. A former colleague found some database work I could do for him and the rest is history.

I did try and think ahead, to me this wasn't a temporary fix, although it could have been. I no longer enjoyed my full time role, it had been diluted so much that it no longer resembled the job I had gone to do, and it no longer challenged me, it bored me if anything. Although this was thrust on me suddenly I saw an opportunity, albeit a far away one, of one day being able to work for myself. Little did I know how quickly that would actually happen.

I chose a business name that would grow as my business evolved, ordered business cards and I set up a basic website.

Thanks to referral my hobby grew, which is a good job really, as just a few months later I was asked to cut my work hours by yet another day. It was an opportunity I had been hoping for as I was doing more work on an evening now as it wouldn't fit into the one day off I already had. And it grew, and it grew. This referral thing was really working for me, and I began to resent every hour I worked in that job that I no longer enjoyed, wishing I was working for me.

Then one day I got the bad news: they wanted me to go back to working four days a week. Well it was bad news to me, they couldn't understand why I wasn't enthusiastic and delighted at the news. Truth was if they had cut my hours I would have been delighted, this was like a death knoll to my hobby. I couldn't see how it could survive if I had to go back to four days, as I was already working well beyond 5 to 9 each day as it was. I had tasted self employment and I wanted more.

I was given a month's reprieve, they honestly thought I would come round to their way of thinking, but the thought of carrying out this diluted role yet another day a week filled me with horror. I had to do something, but what! I had confidence in my hobby, some day it would be a full time business, but it wasn't quite there yet, and with the mortgage and bills to pay there was no way I could afford to take a gamble. It didn't help that several close colleagues had already handed their notice in to go and set up their own businesses, albeit in different fields.

And then I got the phone call, someone was looking for some outside help, would I be interested, they had been referred to me by someone I already worked for. Suddenly my dream was within reach! Before the end of the interview the work was mine. It was enough extra hours each week which meant that I could go for it.

This was a huge, scary step. To go from a guaranteed salary, albeit in a job I really hated by now, to being solely responsible for generating my own salary was an immense jump. I had so much support from my online networks, and even the support of my family, so in the end it wasn't a hard decision. The following day I went in to work and handed my notice in. Simples. The change was instant. Whilst I still had to work a full months notice every one commented that the old Helen was back, they could hear the difference in me, see the difference in me, I was no longer the worn down, diluted person they had come to know, I was back to being me, confident in my abilities and looking forward to getting up each day again.

So on 22nd September HLS Business Solutions celebrates its first full year of trading, no longer a hobby, but a fully fledged business, supporting my family and I, and ensuring that each day I wake up looking forward to work. What more could I ask for!

The story doesn't stop there, though it could, it actually got better. Just a short six months later I started to take on a team of Associates to help with the work load. It also introduced new skills to the team, we all learn from each other, and it makes the business stronger as there is a constant line of support available.

Okay, like most business owners I can't claim to work 9 to 5, some evenings I will still be working at midnight, some mornings I won't start work till 10, and some days I will just take the morning or afternoon off. Because I can. My hobby has become my new career: it pays my mortgage and bills, it allows me to spend quality time with my daughter when it matters, sports day, school trips and yes, even the dreaded recorder recitals!

So don't despair, if you have the right business model, are prepared to put the work in, and perform to the high standards required by your clients then it can happen for you too. I can't say it hasn't been hard work, it has, I have put hours of sweat and blood into this, but you know what? It was worth every minute of it.

The journey has been much faster than I anticipated, and along the way I have encountered some amazing people, not least my clients who I truly love working with. I have learned many new things and made many new friends. And I wouldn't change a minute of it. This roller coaster ride is just beginning and for now I don't want to get off.

When to say goodbye to your clients

When you first start out as a Virtual Assistant it can be very tempting to take on any and all work that comes your way. However, this isn't always the best thing for your business.

I am sure that, like many Virtual Assistants I have spoken with, you will at some point come across a client who is high maintenance or constantly pays their invoices late, perhaps they quibble down to the last minute.

I started to read an interesting book, 'The 4-Hour Work Week: Escape the 9-5, Live Anywhere and Join the New Rich' by Timothy Ferris. Now apart from the fact he suggests outsourcing to a Virtual Assistant who isn't me he made some interesting observations. He referred to the Pareto rule, the 80/20. He looked at what he was doing and found that 80% of what he was doing was only earning him 20% of his income, and it made me think.

I also had a very interesting phone call with Richard White, from The Accidental Salesman, in which we discussed the type of clients I should look to work with.

So what did all this reading and chatting do for me? It made me stop and think about how I wanted to work, what was best for me, and also what was best for my clients. I looked at the clients that I was working with at that time and asked myself if I was really the best solution for that particular client, and if they were the right type of client for me.

When you do your job well as a Virtual Assistant you build up a fantastic relationship with your clients. For some clients you even become that trusted advisor, the one they turn to before they make any decisions, or the person they know they can rely on for that last minute task.

When you first discuss working with a new client listen to your gut instinct. Do you get on. Will you enjoy the work. Are you capable of meeting that clients requirements. Gut instinct may seem a bit chancy to be making important decisions on, but in my two years as a Virtual Assistant I can assure you that it has served more than one VA well.

So what is a high maintenance client? It's someone who has you on speed dial and knows how to use it, whatever time of day or day of the week. It's someone who constantly sends you work with little or no notice that has to be done right now. It's the client who is always ringing up to ask your opinion on everything. Is this a bad thing? Not always, no. But if you have more than one client this can all be to the detriment of our other clients. If this client is your biggest retainer client again it may not be an issue, but typically a high maintenance client will be the one who buys the least hours or pays the lowest rate.

You will find that 80% of your attention is directed to the high maintenance client who actually should only represent 20% of your workload. Sound familiar? It's an easy trap to fall into.

The other thing to beware of is the late payer, or the quibbler. I prefer to offer my clients a healthy discount for buying their hours in advance. They do have the option of paying by invoice each week but this is at a much higher rate. If your shiny new client starts to quibble over your first invoice this is generally a good indication of how they will react to future invoices. Are they dissecting your invoice minute by minute? A healthy interest in how you have spent their money is all well and good but if they are nit picking over 5 minutes here or there despite you using time tracking software then what will they be like when you present your first major invoice. Did they pay their invoice on time, or are there excuses each month when payment should have been made?

Take a moment, step back and review the clients you are currently working with. Do any of the above sound familiar? I do hope not, but if they do, consider whether you should really continue working with them. It's not good for your mental health, and it certainly isn't good for your business.

Whilst the temptation to shoulder the client is there, consider if working with them is stopping you finding the perfect new client that could be out there.

To me a client relationship should be something that you enjoy, not someone who's name appears on your caller ID and you groan. Be honest how many of you have that type of client on your books at the moment? I don't. But it's taken a steep learning curve to reach this point.

As a Virtual Assistant you cannot just think about yourself, you have to consider how this client relationship will affect your other clients and your workload, as well as thinking about your sanity, and ensuring you enjoy your job. After all, isn't part of the reason we became Virtual Assistants that we didn't enjoy our previous roles.

Cutting Costs or Cutting Corners?

There's a temptation when you start your own business to do it on a tight budget, mind you some of us didn't actually have a budget to start with, just a reduced salary, a regular amount of mortgage and bills and the gap between the two! So how do you decide where to spend your hard earned cash, and should you?

The real question here is are you trying to run a professional and legal business or just a hobby? Harsh, perhaps, but you're either doing this for the right reasons or you're playing at it.

Many aspiring to become a Virtual Assistant are led astray by the belief they can just work from their existing home office, this could be true as many home offices are now better equipped than some workplaces I have worked in, however, it's not just about a laptop and a phone line when you consider setting up a business. You cannot compare what you earned in an employed position and just translate that into an hourly rate, there are expenses associated with being in business that you have to account for as well.

There are areas where you cannot and must not scrimp, or go without. These are your professional insurances such as indemnity and liability, your participation in regulatory activities such as registering with the Information Commissioner or HMRC under their Money Laundering Regulations (if you provide any form of bookkeeping service), and having properly licensed software.

These are just a fraction of the things you need to take into account, we'll be covering a lot more of them in future blog posts.

As we have said before in previous posts, don't be tempted to splash the cash because you think you need something either, chances are you probably don't and it will just sit in a corner of your office and haunt you as it gathers dust.

You should have worked out what your business is going to offer clients in terms of services. Look at that list and think about what you will need in order to be able to supply them. Do you need that A3 laminator, that box of envelopes and the fancy letterheads?

Spend your money on items that will either keep your business legal, such as the regulatory stuff above, that will allow you to offer your chosen services or that will allow you to present a professional appearance. You also need to avoid the temptation to use only free products as they are not always the best tool for the job. There are some excellent free tools out there, as well as some low cost ones, you'll have seen our A to Z if you signed up for our newsletter. Don't invest in expensive creative software if you are not planning to offer design services, don't invest in expensive printers if you're not supplying mail shots. Before investing in anything carefully analyse whether the expense will add value to your business or not.

Here's my list of what I think the essential start up items are for a successful Virtual Assistant

1. **Computer** - it's got to be up to the job, you'll be using it all day every day so make sure it has the oomph you need

2. **Dedicated phone number** - please don't put your mobile number as your only point of contact - you can get a free or low cost VoIP phone number that will allow you to divert calls to your mobile or house line if you need, and with the investment in a VoIP handset and call package you can make your calls using this number as well.

3. **Domain name and email address** - there is nothing that screams amateur more than a hotmail or gmail email address. A .co.uk domain name costs less than £10 for 2 years, set up a proper email address as soon as possible.

4. **Insurance** - don't expect that your home office equipment is automatically covered under your home insurance, it may well not be, and remember if you are using your car to drive to meetings or to clients premises you need to add business cover. You need to arrange indemnity insurance to protect your clients and if you have visitors to your business office you will need liability insurance as well.

5. **Professional registrations** with Information Commissioner and HMRC for Money Laundering Regulations if applicable. If you're not sure if you should be registered just pick up the phone and ask

them, from my experience they are human and very helpful!

6. **Website** - with hosting for around £40 year from companies like evohosting (see our tools of the trade page for details) that even include a free domain name you can create your own WordPress website, and have the hosting for your email.

7. **Online profiles** - these cost nothing to set up, just your time, you should have a profile on LinkedIn, Twitter and a Facebook business page (keep your personal and business Facebook separate). Encourage recommendations on LinkedIn, its fantastic advertising if people can see other LinkedIn users have used you and recommend you.

8. **CRM System** - start out now as you mean to go on, CapsuleCRM offers a low cost solution and will integrate with MailChimp for your email marketing, allow you to control your task list, manage your sales pipeline and keep on top of projects. You may think you can manage now just by using Outlook and a calendar but trust me, missing just one follow up could cost you financially. Get into good habits now and as your business grows it will pay dividends.

9. **Bookkeeping** - have a separate bank account from day one, don't mix your business and personal transactions, it will cost you money in the long term trying to sort it all out. If you are going to want to pay for items or accept payment for invoices by PayPal then set up your account now and use your new

business email address to keep it separate from your personal account.

10. **Support network** - Going from a busy office environment to suddenly working alone can be intimidating, lonely and scary, let's add into the equation the fact you've possibly no experience of running a business and it can quickly get overwhelming. Find the support networks that are out there, join them and use them! The amount of support and knowledge out there is amazing and it costs little or nothing to join.

11. **Knowledge!** Without this you cannot run your business, and please note I am using the word knowledge not qualifications or certificates, do you posess the knowledge to offer the services you are providing, a potential client won't be hung up on pretty pieces of paper, they just care whether you can produce the goods or not.

Don't put all your eggs in one basket

It's really comforting when you start your Virtual Assistant business and you land a flagship client, the client who takes up the majority of your time, has guaranteed you a large number of hours per month.

However, what happens when you lose that client? If you're doing your job well then it could happen. That's right, by doing your job well you can lose clients! You help your client grow their business so successfully that they now require premises and a full time member of staff on site.

Whilst it's flattering that you have helped your client grow and succeed in their business, this can have a massively detrimental effect on your own business. It's not just in terms of lost earnings, but it can have a psychological effect as well.

It's important that when this happens both sides manage the situation, and especially communicate the reason that the partnership has broken up. Too often others assume it's the Virtual Assistant who has failed to perform, when in actuality, it's the very same Virtual Assistant's competency that has resulted in this change.

Having a client out grow you does leave you with a feeling of loss, quite often clients become good friends and it's hard to take a step back when you've been used to constant contact.

The most important thing however, is not to forget to market your business whilst you have your flagship client. If you lost your main client could your business afford to continue?

Don't become complacent in your business, continue to investigate new opportunities, spread yourself out amongst several clients, continue to learn, and keep growing your business.

Social Media - When you shouldn't be social

Anyone who knows me knows that I am a social media addict, I've been on Twitter for four years now and have my regular daily fix, or rather several daily fixes and I'm the same with Facebook. I firmly believe that if we use Social Media in the right way then it can only help us to grow our business.

But that's not what today's post is about, this post is about when using Social Media can go wrong.

It was prompted by a recent private Facebook group post from someone telling us they'd lost their job as a result of a comment they made on Social Media, Facebook to be specific. This comment should only have been available to friends, but one of those so called friends brought the comment to the attention of the employer and... a job was lost.

In another instance, again involving Facebook, a comment made in a closed group was shared outside of the group, not only breaking the trust of the group, but again causing a great deal of distress and unnecessary suffering.

Facebook has groups, personal pages and business pages for a reason. It's so that you don't mix when you shouldn't. I know I am as guilty as anyone on there of accepting a friend request when in reality I should have directed someone to my author page or business page, or perhaps it's a friend of a friend that I don't know that well. But, as a result of that I am careful what I say and where I say it.

Just because you would never dream of sharing a private confidence doesn't mean that someone else would think twice about it. Before you type something make sure that you are happy for that to be broadcast or read by others. Also remember that a comment taken out of context can mean something totally different to someone else who reads it.

You may make an innocent remark, no specific person in mind when it's said, but someone reads it and perceives it to be a veiled insult to them. It happens.

Whilst Facebook posts should only appear to the people you have given permission to, we nearly all have phones that take screen shots, we all know how to copy and paste. Do you really want to say what you were going to say now?

If you use a medium such as Twitter then you need to remember ANYONE can read your post, and Google helpfully scans and records it all for posterity. You've all probably read of innocently meant remarks that ended up in court cases.

The worst crime for me in Social Media is when you post a message when you're either drunk, or emotionally not in the right frame of mind. Think about how what you say will reflect on people's opinion of you when they read it stone cold sober. Was that really the impression of you that you wanted to portray?

So by all means have a laugh on social media, and share what you want to share, but before you press post or submit have another look at what you've written and ask yourself if that's really what you wanted to say. *(and don't forget to check your spelling!)*

You get what you pay for

I had a phone conversation when the caller mentioned a picture I had shared on Facebook. They were commenting how true they felt it was, it was about getting what you paid for. It was an image that a friend had seen shared on LinkedIn, a sign in a shop window that stated:

We offer three kinds of service:

Good - Cheap - Fast

You can pick any TWO
GOOD service CHEAP won't be FAST
GOOD service FAST won't be CHEAP
FAST service CHEAP won't be GOOD

This applies to all aspects of your business. It applies to the rate you charge your customers for your product or service, and also the rate you pay your suppliers for your product or service.

Let's face it, the supermarkets have been offering this for years now in the guise of their value, standard and extra special ranges. We all understand that if we want the extra special then there is a premium to pay, and that if we choose value then it won't be as good as the extra special.

Whilst I am the first to look for a bargain, I am a tight Yorkshire lass after all, I also believe in value for money.

Working in a service industry I often see people concentrate on an hourly rate and try to beat it down as low as they can, without actually seeing what they are getting. Sure I can work for you for a lower rate, but would you honestly expect that you'd get my full service and attention? My rate isn't just about the time it takes me to do a job, which thanks to my experience could well be a lot less time than someone less experienced and cheaper, you're paying for the knowledge, the workmanship, the experience and the added value that comes from working with me.

When you buy a new product for your home you want something that will last. I don't know about you but I go for the product that I can afford, even if that's the top end of my budget, that will last and actually do what I need it to do. There's no point in me buying something cheap when I know that in just a few months I'll have to replace it, I'd rather invest the money and get a product that will last or do the job properly.

I see this more and more on behalf of clients in the current climate, they'll send a quote out which covers a professional and quality service only for the end user to choose the cheapest quote, which then doesn't do what they expected, and call my client back asking them to fix it.

When you ask someone to discount their rate then you must also accept that there will be a reduction in the service or product to allow for that. Let's use a hot chocolate as an example, the value version is an instant hot chocolate, the standard version is a hot chocolate made with fresh hot milk, and the deluxe is a hot chocolate made with fresh hot milk and added cream and marshmallows. When you walk into the coffee shop you accept that there are variable prices depending on the quality or size of the product that you have chosen. Why then do people not transfer this logic into their buying and selling decisions?

If you're a supplier then have a look at what you offer, if you're offering a discount or reduction can you justify that in terms of a reduction in the product or service as well? If you're a buyer are you sure that the budget option actually represents the best value over a period of time or will it prove, in the end, to be false economy?

About Helen Stothard

I have over twenty years experience of helping business efficiently organise and complete their administration. In 2009, I set up HLS Business Solutions to offer a virtual Executive Business Assistance service to coaches, trainers and consultants.

I am known for my pragmatic outlook and Yorkshire spirit – and am regularly in demand for ideas and inspiration on how to improve administrative processes and implement social media within the business marketing mix.

I am told I am an inspiration to many virtual assistants and people running a 5-9 business. I am one of the few people who have successfully made the jump from a 5-9 business to a 9-5 business. After only six months of running HLS Business Solutions, my proactive service and high standards were so much in demand, that HLS Business Solutions added in four team members – enabling HLS Business solutions to deliver a full virtual executive assistance service.

I am a straight talking northern lass, mother to one, a business owner, coffee drinker, cat food provider, good friend, enthusiastic but slow runner, an avid reader and a twitter addict, not necessarily in that order.

I have never once regretted making the jump from corporate life to running my own business, I love it. Working from home allows me the time to be mum at the school gate and still get the buzz I need to be me (as well as pay the bills).

Contact Helen Stothard

Helen Stothard

HLS Business Solutions

Tel: 01904 890212

Email:

helen@hlsbs.co.uk

Web and Business Blogs:

http://www.hlsbs.com (HLS Business Solutions)

http://www.trainingforvas.com (intelligentVA)

Skype:

hstothard

Twitter:

http://www.twitter.com/helenstothard

LinkedIn:

http://uk.linkedin.com/in/helenstothard

Facebook:

http://www.facebook.com/hlsbusiness

Personal Blogs:

http://www.helenstothard.com

http://www.runfatgirlrun.co.uk

Other books by Helen Stothard

The A to Z of Virtual Assistant Tools

This is a directory of some of the tools that I use in the day to day running of my Virtual Assistant (VA) business. These are the tools that save me time, make me more efficient for my clients and help me run my business more smoothly.

This book is designed to help Virtual Assistants at all stages of their career; for those who are just starting out I hope this will give some idea of the resources available to assist in your future ventures, and for those who have been working as a Virtual Assistant for a while, I hope these tools will help you streamline both your client and business tasks, to save time in all aspects of your organisation.

The Virtual Assistant Tools in this book range from information for you to consider during the set-up process, to online resources to assist you with the running of your business. Furthermore, most of them are free, or offer a trial version, so you can try them and experience how they can work for you.

As you can imagine, there are many more resources available than are listed in this book. In the A to Z of Virtual Assistant Tools, I've listed the ones that are my favourites; I love to use them and they have had the biggest positive impact on my business.

How to get started on

twitter

& Generate Business

by Helen Stothard

How to get started on Twitter and generate business

You know you need to be on Twitter but you still don't "get it". Neither did I. I was a Facebook gal, through and through, how on earth could I communicate in just 140 characters? I was used to a whole Facebook status to play with, and couldn't see how it could work.

So, how am I qualified to write this book? I'm not really, I'm just a simple northern lass who found a way to make Twitter work for her, and it's that journey that I am going to share here with you. I'm not saying that this will work for everyone, but it has worked for me, and if nothing else, it will help take some of the mystery out of Twitter for you. I would however like to point out that in the space of just a few months I personally had six Clients who could all be attributed to Twitter and this number has grown considerably since then, I know of other contacts who have also had success with Twitter, so I am talking from direct experience here, I would say over 90% of my business can now be attributed back to Twitter.

"Helen Stothard's 'I Don't Get Twitter' guide coaxed me gently and logically into the wonderful world of Twitter. Written in no-nonsense, plain speaking English, it guided me through those crucial 'getting started' steps, to a clear understanding of Twitter activity. It's a fab guide for Twitter

novices looking for a 'way in' and I wholeheartedly recommend it."

Victoria Clarke, January 2011

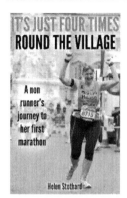

It's just four times round the Village

A non runner's journey to her first marathon.

Running a marathon can seem overwhelming but 'it's just four times round the village'.

This isn't your normal journey to a marathon.

For over 16 years I'd been a contented sofa surfer; I was overweight and very unfit when I agreed to take on my first 10k after a light hearted challenge from my brother.

That first step would eventually lead me to fulfil one of my childhood dreams - taking part in the London Marathon.

'It's just four times round the village' takes you on my five year journey, sharing the ups and the downs along the way, and is for those of you dreaming of running London Marathon from the comfort of your armchair, people like me who don't have the natural inclination to run, and those surrounded by people telling you that you can't or you shouldn't.

Because there is one thing that I have learned, if I can do it, then anyone can!

If you've enjoyed this book I'd be really
grateful if you could leave a review for me
over at either Amazon or Goodreads

http://www.amazon.co.uk/Setting-Assistant-Challenge-Challenges-
ebook

http://www.goodreads.com/book/show/18398367-30-day-setting-
up-as-a-virtual-assistant-challenge

Printed in Great Britain
by Amazon